Christmas

make me I'm yours...

D&C
David and Charles
www.rucraft.co.uk

A DAVID & CHARLES BOOK

Copyright © David & Charles Limited 2010

David & Charles is an F+W Media Inc. company
4700 East Galbraith Road, Cincinnati,
OH 45236

First published in the UK and US in 2010

Text and designs copyright © Dorothy Wood,
Marion Elliot, Elizabeth Moad, Lindy Smith,
Joan & Graham Belgrove, Ellen Kharade,
Mandy Shaw, Alice Butcher & Ginny Farquhar,
Barri Sue Gaudet, Helen Philipps 2010

Layout and photography copyright
© David & Charles Limited 2010

Dorothy Wood, Marion Elliot, Elizabeth
Moad, Lindy Smith, Joan & Graham Belgrove,
Ellen Kharade, Mandy Shaw, Alice Butcher
& Ginny Farquhar, Barri Sue Gaudet,
Helen Philipps have asserted their rights
to be identified as authors of this work in
accordance with the Copyright, Designs and
Patents Act, 1988.

A catalogue record for this book is available
from the British Library.

ISBN-13: 978-0-7153-3896-4 hardback
ISBN-10: 0-7153-3896-X hardback

Printed in the UK by Butler, Tanner & Dennis Ltd.
for David & Charles
Brunel House, Newton Abbot, Devon

Acquisitions Editor Cheryl Brown
Assistant Editor Jeni Hennah
Editorial Assistant Kate Daniel
Project Editor Alison Smith
Design Manager Sarah Clark
Art Editor Kevin Mansfield
Photographers Kim Sayer, Karl Adamson,
Lorna Yabsley, Ginette Chapman, Simon
Whitmore, Sian Irvine and Joe Giacomet
Production Controller Kelly Smith
Pre Press Jodie Culpin and Natasha Jorden

David & Charles publish high quality books
on a wide range of subjects. For more great
book ideas visit: **www.rucraft.co.uk**

contents

introduction

The weeks leading up to Christmas are an inspiring time because the shops are filled with so many gorgeous items, and the displays are so wonderful. It is tempting simply to buy everything you need, but where's the fun in that? It's much more satisfying, and a lot of fun, to make your own creations! Friends and family will love a handmade present, card or treat, and visitors to your home will admire your beautiful decorations.

Make Me I'm Yours... Christmas includes irresistible festive baking, beading, needlecraft and papercraft projects, some quick and others more detailed. It's full of ideas that will hopefully inspire you to create your own variations, as the huge choice of beads, fabrics, papers and embellishments is a constant source of delight.

Each project lists the materials you will need and offers clear step-by-step instructions to guide you through. Many of the projects have variations which offer simpler versions of the main project that use quicker methods or alternative materials and will help to give you the confidence to embark on more complex projects or your own designs.

The techniques section that begins on page 86, together with the useful tips, will help you along the way. So what are you waiting for — choose a project, collect your materials and start creating today!

holly wreath

A lovely Christmas tradition is to hang a holly wreath from the front door to welcome your visitors, so why not create an indoor version that could be hung from a door or on the wall and used year after year as part of your festive decorations. This contemporary holly wreath uses a beautiful green printed silk for the leaves, embellished with a colourful selection of buttons and beads. This is certain to become a favourite piece and something you look forward to putting up every year.

The base of the wreath is very simple to make and you can easily add variety by using an assortment of buttons. For a less traditional look, try using different colours for the leaves.

you will need ...

- ★ 4m (157½in) millinery wire
- ★ 12 x 120cm (4¾ x 47in) approx. wadding
- ★ 12 x 120cm (4¾ x 47in)
- ★ green linen
- ★ wire cutters
- ★ small round-nose pliers
- ★ 30–40 green buttons
- ★ scrap of red felt
- ★ 25 x 112cm (9¾ x 44¼in)
- ★ medium-weight printed cotton
- ★ or silk for leaves
- ★ 21 red, berry-like beads
- ★ green and red multi-purpose sewing threads
- ★ small quantity of toy stuffing
- ★ 25 x 120cm (9¾ x 47in)
- ★ green felt for leaves
- ★ masking tape
- ★ 20cm (8in) green bias binding

form the wire base ...

1 Taking one end of the millinery wire, shape a 28cm (11in) diameter circle and fasten the end with masking tape. Continue to wind around the remaining wire to create a firm ring. Wrap this closely together with masking tape, which will be covered.

2 To create the hanging loop, cut 30cm (12in) of millinery wire and wind one end tightly to the wire wreath base using pliers. Form a loop with the next 12–14cm (4¾–5½in) of wire. Fasten back to the wreath base with a couple of turns. Then pull the loop a little closer together and twist the remaining wire around to hold secure **(a)**. Wrap a small strip of bias binding around the loop and secure with a couple of stitches.

a

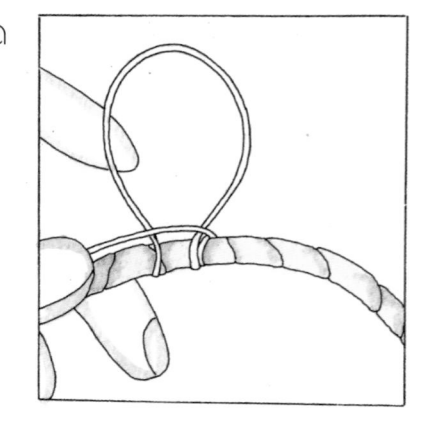

b

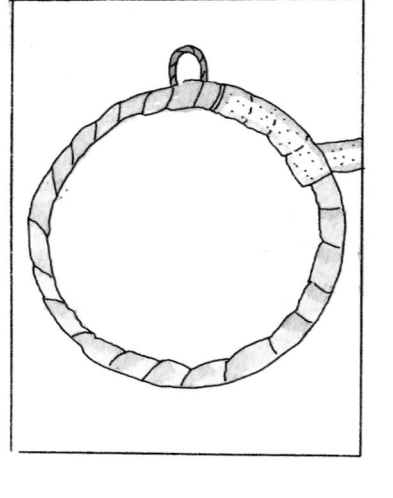

3 Cut three widths of wadding 4cm (1½in) wide and wind evenly around the wreath base, joining on more as necessary with a couple of stitches. Secure at the end (**b**).

You could wind 2 or 3 different coloured linens around the wreath base to create a striped effect.

c

4 Cut the green linen into three pieces on the straight grain, each 4 x 120cm (1½ x 47in) and join together along the short edges. Machine topstitch 2mm (¾in) from the left-hand edge along the entire strip. Fray the edge back just shy of the stitch line. Starting at the loop, attach the strip to the wadding with a couple of stitches and start to wind clockwise around the wreath base, covering the raw edge and leaving the frayed edge visible (**c**).

make the holly leaves …

1 Cut out 21 leaf shapes using the templates and pin wrong sides together on to your felt backing. Stitch just inside the edge of each leaf, leaving a small opening for the stuffing. Cut out, lightly stuff and machine stitch the gap closed. Zigzag over the raw edges to neaten. Highlight the central vein with a backstitch in green embroidery thread.

2 Take three leaves and sew together with a few stab stitches. Cut out 21 red felt circles between 1cm (⅜in) and 2cm (¾in) diameter for the berries. Attach to the trio of leaves with a cross-stitch and finish with a red ceramic bead **(d)**. Position these arrangements in clusters around the main wreath. Pin and stitch by hand. To complete your wreath, sew green buttons between the holly leaves.

d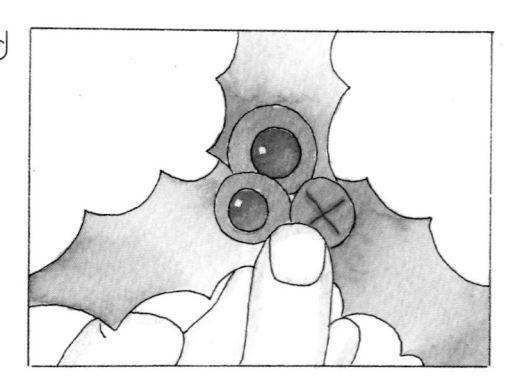

As an alternative to linen, satin and silky fabrics make a luxurious base for your wreath. Allow the fabric to curve gently and find its own natural position rather than pulling taught.

techniques basic sewing kit p. 88 ... using a sewing machine p. 93 ... topstitch p. 95 ... zigazag stitch p. 95 ...
backstitch p. 101 ... sewing on buttons p. 104 *templates* p. 110

holly wreath 11

Christmas countdown

Every family member will know it's Christmas time when this charming advent calendar is hung. This timeless keepsake will last for years but should take only a week to complete. Allow three or four days to make the pockets and three more days for assembly of the back and borders. Then choose special treats and gifts to slot into the beautifully decorated pockets and surprise your loved ones every day of advent.

Adorable little angels, candy canes, hearts and candles are just some of the enchanting motifs that give this wallhanging its festive charm.

you will need ...

★ 91.4 x 111.8cm (36 x 44in) ecru flannel for pockets and borders

★ 30.5 x 111.8cm (12 x 44in) light green fabric for borders

★ 30.5 x 111.8cm (12 x 44in) red fabric for borders and tabs

★ 58.4 x 61cm (23 x 24in) backing fabric

★ 38.1 x 38.1cm (15 x 15in) white wool felt

★ 25.4 x 25.4cm (10 x 10in) wool felt in red, green, yellow, blue, brown and peach

★ 40.6 x 40.6cm (16 x 16in) freezer paper

★ 91.4 x 45.7cm (36 x 18in) medium-weight fusible interfacing

★ 61 x 58.4cm (24 x 23in) lightweight wadding (batting)

★ embroidery thread (floss)

★ glue or 15.2 x 15.2cm (6 x 6in) double-sided fusible webbing

1 Cut out 25 12.7 x 8.9cm (5 x 3½in) pieces of ecru fabric for the pocket fronts. Fold each in half wrong sides together so that each front is 6.4 x 8.9cm (2½ x 3½in). Attach a 5.7 x 7.6cm (2¼ x 3in) piece of fusible interfacing to one side of this folded piece to add strength. This is the side you appliqué.

2 Following the template, trace the scalloped piece on to freezer paper and then iron to the white wool felt. Cut out 25 pieces. Repeat for the festive designs but using the wool felt colours. There are three snowmen, three hearts, three stars, three candles, two trees, two baubles, two reindeer, two candy canes, two angels, two stockings, and one Santa Claus.

3 Trace from the template or embroider the designs freehand on to the scalloped pieces and festive designs following the motif guide on pages 16–17. Glue the wool felt appliqué pieces in place on the pocket fronts. Be careful not to let your designs go past the 6mm (¼in) seam allowance along the bottom edge. The scalloped top should be level with the fold in the fabric, and the designs in the middle of each pocket.

4 Whipstitch the wool felt appliqué pieces to the pocket fronts using one strand of matching embroidery thread being careful not to catch the back of the fold in the stitching. This is meant to fold over and line the backs of the pockets to cover the knots and threads.

5 Cut out 25 pocket backs out of ecru fabric 8.9 x 8.9cm (3½ x 3½in). Pin or baste the pocket front (back folded down) to each back with the bottom and side edges even. 2.5cm (1in) should be left on top for more embroidery.

6 Cut 20 8.9 x 2.5cm (3½ x 1in) pieces of the light green fabric. Sew one of these through all the layers to the right side of the first four pockets in each row. The fifth pocket in each row will have a joining border later. Join these pockets together into rows by sewing the left side of pockets two to five to the right side of pockets one to four in each row. Press the seams towards the light green border.

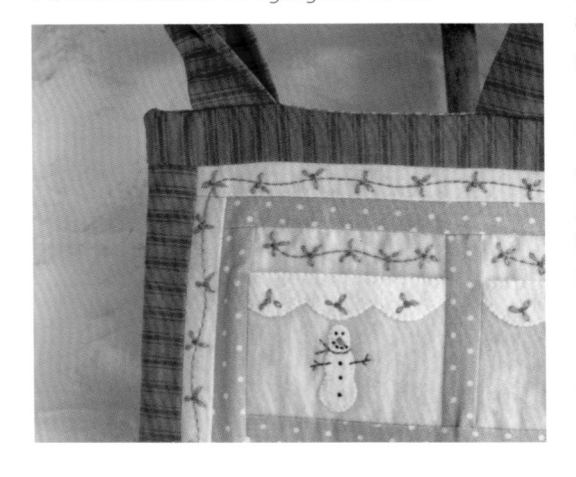

7 Cut four 3.8 x 43.2cm (1½ x 17in) strips of the light green fabric for the horizontal borders. Join the rows together leaving the first row free of a top horizontal strip and the fifth row free of a bottom horizontal strip. Press seams towards the light green borders.

8 Cut two 49.5 x 2.5cm (19½ x 1in) strips of the light green fabric for the side borders. Sew to the sides, and press seams open. Cut two 2.5 x 47cm (1 x 18½in) strips from the same fabric and sew to the top and bottom. Press seams open.

9 Cut two 52.1 x 2.5cm (20½ x 1in) strips of the ecru flannel. Sew to the sides and press seams open. Cut two 2.5 x 49.5cm (1 x 19½in) strips of the same fabric. Sew to the top and bottom and press the seams.

10 Cut two 54.6 x 3.8cm (21½ x 1½in) strips of the red fabric for the final border. Sew to the sides and press seams open. Cut two 3.8 x 54.6cm (1½ x 21½in) strips of the same fabric. Sew to the top and bottom and press open.

11 Using a wash-away pen trace embroidery lines to the remaining 2.5cm (1in) top of each pocket and the ecru border, following the template.

12 Attach lightweight wadding to the back by pinning, tacking or with fabric adhesive to create a quilted effect while stitching. Stitch embroidery work following the guide.

13 Remove any tracing lines with a damp sponge.

14 Cut five 15.2 x 8.9cm (6 x 3½in) strips of red fabric. Fold each in half along the 15.2cm (6in) edge, right sides together. Sew this edge, turn right side out and press. Fold in half to create a loop, and pin or tack the tabs along the top edge.

15 With right sides together, sew the 58.4 x 61cm (23 x 24in) piece of backing fabric to the front, leaving an opening for turning. Clip the corners and trim edges to 6mm (¼in). Turn right side out and whipstitch the opening closed to finish the project.

16 To decorate the border, backstitch the vines with two strands of green. Lazy daisy stitch the holly leaves with two strands of green and add french knots with three strands of red for the berries.

Motifs

- **Snowman:** backstitch the nose with two strands of orange. French knot eyes, mouth and buttons with one strand of black. Backstitch the arms with two strands of brown. Backstitch the scarf with two strands of blue **(a)**.
- **Heart:** French knot dots all round with three strands of pink **(b)**.
- **Star:** French knot a berry in the centre with three strands of red. Lazy daisy stitch the leaves with two strands of green. French knot dots at the points with three strands of yellow **(c)**.
- **Tree:** backstitch the garland with three strands of yellow. French knot the dot on the top of the tree with three strands of yellow. French knot the tree ornaments with three strands of blue **(d)**.
- **Candles:** French knot the berries with three strands of red. Lazy daisy stitch the leaves with two strands of green. Backstitch the flame highlights with two strands of orange. Backstitch the candlewicks with one strand of black **(e)**.
- **Bauble:** backstitch the stars with two strands of white. French knot the dots with three strands of yellow. Backstitch the top of the bauble with three strands of grey. Backstitch the hanger with one strand of black **(f)**.
- **Candy canes:** backstitch the stripes with three strands of red. Tie a bow around the centre and secure with glue **(g)**.

- **Reindeer:** backstitch the antlers and legs with two strands of brown. Lazy daisy stitch the ears and tail with two strands of brown. French knot the nose with two strands of brown. Backstitch the collar with two strands of red. French knot the bells on the collar with two strands of yellow. French knot the eyes with one strand of black **(h)**.

- **Angel:** backstitch the halo with three strands of yellow. French knot the dots on the dress with three strands of yellow. Backstitch the arms and legs with three strands of peach **(i)**.

- **Stocking:** French knot the dots with three strands of red.

- **Santa Claus:** lazy daisy stitch the moustache with three strands of white. French knot the eyes with one strand of black.

techniques basic sewing kit p. 88 ... backstitch p. 101 ... lazy daisy p. 101 ... French knot p. 103 ... catch stitch p. 101
templates p. 110

gingerbread toys

These cute cookie-shaped toys make lovely decorations for the kitchen or children's bedrooms at Christmas. You could make Mr and Mrs Gingerbread, as shown here, or create a whole family and decorate each one slightly differently using a variety of different fabrics, ribbons, buttons and other embellishments. If you're feeling ambitious, you could even create 'different flavours' by using alternative colours of fabric!

The rich ginger-coloured linen and red and white trimmings reflect the warm, festive and homely joys of the season.

you will need ...

- ★ 2 pieces of 21.5 x 35.5cm (8½ x 14in) 28-count linen in ginger brown
- ★ 35.5 x 6.5cm (14 x 2½in)
- ★ 28-count linen in white for the apron
- ★ DMC stranded cotton 3328
- ★ tapestry needle size 24–26
- ★ polyester toy stuffing
- ★ white acrylic paint
- ★ two white buttons
- ★ two red heart buttons
- ★ red and white check ribbon
- ★ narrow red ribbon
- ★ narrow white ribbon
- ★ tiny white bow
- ★ small bundle of cinnamon sticks (optional)
- ★ doll's cookie cutter (optional)

making mr gingerbread ...

1 Fold the linen in half and trace the template of the body shape on to it (**a**). Cross stitch a tiny heart on the front over two threads of linen using two strands of stranded cotton. Do not cut out the shape yet. Sew round the shape following the chart below (**b**), and then cut it out and clip the curves. Cut a slit in the centre of the back for turning through.

a

b

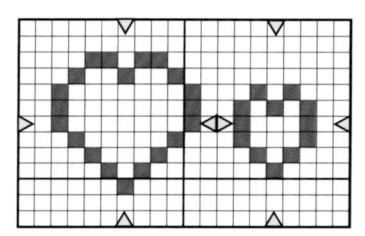

A single cross stitch

Stitch counts: Large 9h x 9w; Small 6h x 5w

Design sizes: Large 2 x 2cm (¾ x ¾in); Small 1.3 x 0.6cm (½ x ¼in)

2 Turn right side out, press and then stuff with polyester stuffing and sew up the gap (**c**).

c

3 Create the face using French knots and black stranded cotton for the eyes, white cotton and backstitch for the mouth. Brush on a little white acrylic paint for the cheeks and dot of white paint for the nose.

4 Using red stranded cotton, sew on the two white buttons on the front.

5 Tie the red and white check ribbon around his neck in a bow. Tie the cinnamon sticks in a bundle with narrow red ribbon (**d**) and tie to the left hand.

d

Why not also make gingerbread cookies? Put them in a cellophane bag tied with a ribbon and place them in a box with a gingerbread toy as a festive gift.

making mrs gingerbread ...

1 Follow steps 1 to 3 for making Mr Gingerbread but do not cross stitch a heart on the body.

2 Make the apron by cutting a 28 x 6cm (11 x 2½in) piece of white linen for the skirt. Sew a seam up the back and hem the bottom by turning up and stitching with red running stitch. Sew a red cross-stitch heart from the chart on page 20, working over two threads of linen with two strands of stranded cotton (**e**).

e

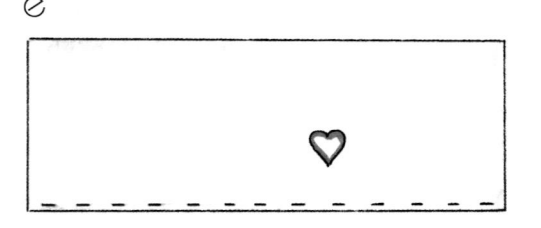

Try adding your own embroidery or cross stitch designs to personalise the apron.

3 To make the top of the apron cut a piece of linen 6.5 x 6.5cm (2½ x 2½in), turn in three sides, press and then catch down with white running stitch (**f**).

f

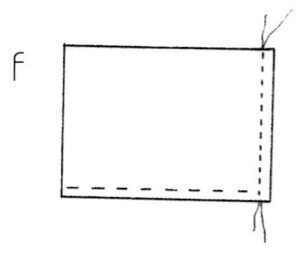

4 Place the top behind the skirt and fit the skirt to the toy by making tucks all round the top. Sew the apron top to the skirt. Make straps using thin white ribbon and sew to the front of the apron in the top right and left corners. Cross the ribbons at the back and sew them to the skirt. Sew red buttons to the apron top with white thread (**g**).

g

5 Sew the tiny white bow to the top of her head. To finish, sew on the cookie cutter to the right hand using matching thread.

You could also make padded hearts and stars from the same linen and add loops so they can hang on the tree.

techniques basic sewing kit p. 88 ... sewing on buttons p. 104 ... French knots p. 103 ... running stitch p. 100 ... backstitch p. 101 *templates* p. 111

heavenly angel

As well as being a favourite Christmas tree adornment, the angel is a symbol of peace, hope and tranquillity. She is made from calico with jute twine hair and her dress is made with linen and lace fabrics using crazy patchwork – a technique of placing fabrics side by side to create wonderful patterns and textures. A beautiful wire halo and golden wings add the finishing touches. With a handy loop at the neck, she can be displayed in pride of place at the top of your tree.

Small embroidered stars, feather stitch and lazy daisies have been used to decorate the skirt. You can personalize your angel by using a variety of decorative stitches.

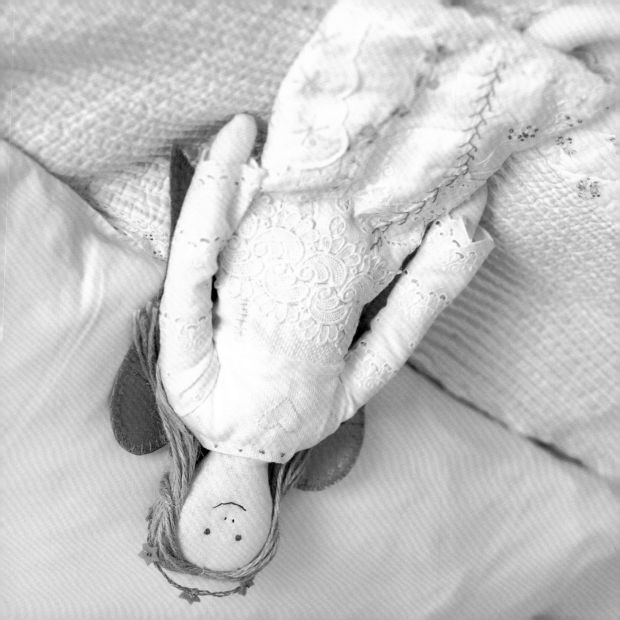

you will need ...

★ 50cm (20in) calico for doll body

★ a variety of vintage linens, tea tray cloths, laces and trims for crazy patchwork

★ 30 x 45cm (12 x 17¾in) white linen for skirt

★ 25cm (9¾in) lace to cover centre back seam

★ 20cm (8in) white velvet ribbon for waistband

★ 20cm (8in) bias binding for neck of dress

★ 30 x 12cm (12 x 4¾in) plain linen for bodice

★ 20 x 40cm (8 x 15¾in) decorative broderie anglaise for sleeves

★ 25 x 20cm (9¾ x 8in) gold felt for wings

★ 50 x 20cm (20 x 8in) gold doupion for wings

★ four 50cm (20in) lengths of twine

★ twenty-six 42cm (16½in) lengths of twine

★ toy stuffing

★ double-sided fusible webbing (Bondaweb)

★ embroidery threads for embellishment

★ 70cm (27½in) thin gold jewellery wire for halo

★ scrap of gold felt for stars on halo

★ five tiny gold beads

construct the body ...

1 Scale up the patterns and transfer to pattern paper. Pin and cut out the pieces for the dolls body and transfer all markings. With right sides together, pin and stitch the main body at the shoulders and side seams from the balance mark. Press the seams open. With right sides together, pin and stitch the legs, arm and head pieces. Trim and clip. Turn through and press. Stuff the legs fully and stitch across the top on the seam allowance to enclose the ends. Stuff the arms firmly but not fully yet. Do not enclose end.

2 Take the main body and insert the unstuffed head into the neck opening right sides together, matching up at the side seams. Pin and hand sew these together with a strong, small backstitch (double thread) on the seam allowance line. Turn through and press. Press under the seam allowance on the main body at the sleeve opening and the leg opening. This gives you a good edge for attaching the limb pieces later. Stuff firmly into the head and lightly into the main body.

3 Insert the arms and pin, making sure to line up the side seams at the armpit and shoulder seam. Sew all the way round with a small backstitch **(a)**. Stuff well into the arms and shoulders and finish stuffing the body fully.

4 Pin the centre point between the two leg openings and insert the legs, ensuring they are the same length. Pin in place and stab stitch through to secure **(b)**.

b

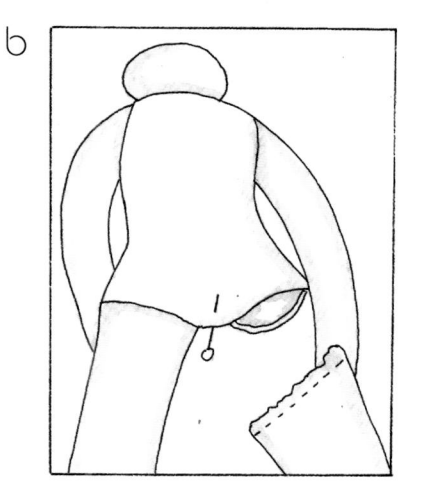

a

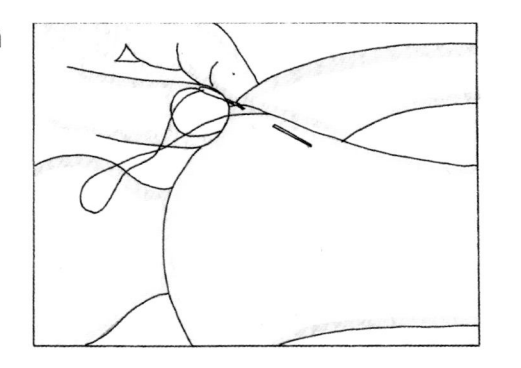

A rouleaux turner is a good way to turn through the slim leg and arm pieces.

add the hair and face ...

1 Take the four longer strands of twine. Fold in half to find the midpoint and, with a double thread, attach to the front of the centre hairline, one at a time with a backstitch **(c)**. Using the 26 shorter lengths continue working towards the back in the same way, one at a time following the centre back until all the head is covered.

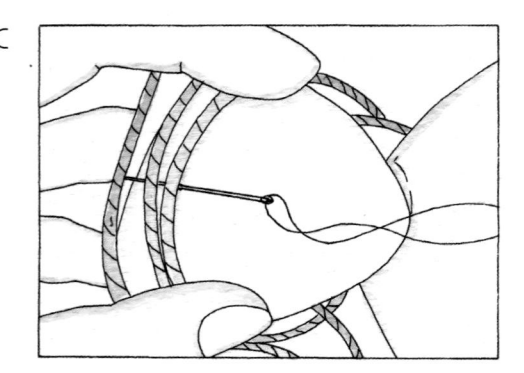

You could replace the twine for the hair with wool if you prefer. You could also change the colour of the fabrics used for the clothes or the shape of the wings.

2 Leaving the front four lengths loose and starting from strand five, secure at the side seams and stitch across the head **(d)**.

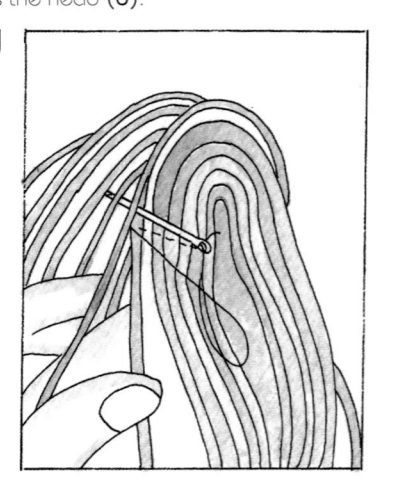

3 Take the front four lengths and twist lightly backwards towards the head. Take these around to the back and secure in a loose ponytail with a few stitches. Secure at the sides if necessary, too. Trim the hair.

4 Draw on your face with a fine, soft chalk pencil. Using normal sewing thread, embroider the eyes with an overstitch, the nose with two tiny French knots and the mouth with backstitch.

make the dress …

1 Cut out the skirt pattern in your white linen cloth and, with right sides together, sew up the side seams but leave the back open. Press and neaten the seams. Lay your skirt flat, ready to apply the crazy patchwork.

2 Follow the instructions on page 107 for crazy patchwork. Have some fun, letting your fabrics lead you, and don't worry if there are a few raw areas as you can embellish over these later.

3 Once you have covered your base cloth, embellish to your heart's content, using the embroidery threads and beads and a variety of stitches. When your patchwork is complete, with right sides together, pin the two edges of the skirt to create the centre back seam. Stitch, neaten, turn and press. Stitch on a lace trim to hide the back seam. Using a pretty trim, edge the bottom hem of the doll's skirt to finish off and embellish as desired.

4 To make up the bodice, cut the main body pieces in plain fabric and with right sides together stitch side and shoulder seams. Neaten seams, centre back and hem edges with a tiny zigzag, press

and turn. Neaten the raw neck edge by applying a bias binding facing. With right sides together, stitch your binding to the neck edge. Clip curves, turn facing to the inside of bodice and press. Slipstitch to secure. Press seam allowance under on the right hand back piece.

5 Cut out the sleeves in a pretty broderie anglaise fabric using the decorative edge as the sleeve hem. With a long stitch approx 4–5mm ($5/32$–$3/16$in) and without double backing, machine stitch a row of stitches to gather up at the sleeve head. With right sides together, sew the side seams, press and neaten. Insert the sleeve into the bodice, easing the gathers in, pin and hand stitch with a small backstitch. Neaten and turn to the right side.

6 With right sides together, attach the bodice to the skirt at the waist, press and neaten. Cover the join with a pretty piece of thin velvet ribbon and embroider French knots around the neck opening and embroider a heart on the front with a tiny running stitch. Dress your doll and secure the bodice back seam with an overstitch.

sew the wings ...

1 Take a piece of Bondaweb approx. 50 x 20cm (20 x 8in) and fuse on to the doupion. Peel off the paper and place the felt on to one half of the doupion (Bondaweb side up). Fold the other half of doupion over the felt and fuse. You now have a sandwich of doupion on either side with the felt in the middle. Trace the wing pattern, pin to the doupion sandwich and cut out. Using the photo opposite for guidance, transfer the stitched wing detail and sew with a machine straight stitch or hand stem stitch. Neaten the edge with zigzag and finally finish with a small blanket stitch in complementary embroidery thread. Highlight the stitching with beads.

2 Fold a 10cm (4in) piece of velvet ribbon in half to create a hanging loop and attach with an overstitch to the centre back of the doll (approx. 3cm (1⅛in) from the neck edge).

3 Pin the wings to the centre back of the doll, concealing the edge of the ribbon, and backstitch into position. Finally, oversew across the centre bottom of the wings to create dimension.

coil the halo ...

Take the gold wire and coil it around twice to fit the dolls head. Wind the rest in and out of the circle to give a wreath-like effect. Cut five tiny felt stars and sew a bead on the centre of each. Sew at regular intervals around the halo ensuring one is placed at the front. Attach the halo to the dolls head at either side and at the centre back.

cookie centrepiece

These elegant snowflake cookies make an attractive table centrepiece, or would look great hanging from your tree. You can use an assortment of different cookie cutters to create different shapes and sizes. The piped white royal icing designs give a gorgeous wintery effect, but you could use different colours and decorations for a brighter Christmas theme.

Silver sugar balls and edible hologram dust add extra sparkle to these delicate snowflake cookies.

you will need ...

for the vanilla cookies ...

- ★ 275g (10oz) plain flour, sifted
- ★ 5ml (1 tsp) baking powder
- ★ 100g (3½ oz) caster sugar
- ★ 75g (3oz) butter, diced
- ★ 1 small egg, beaten
- ★ 30ml (2 tbsp) golden syrup
- ★ 2.5ml (½ tsp) vanilla extract
- ★ snowflake cookie cutters

for decorating ...

- ★ royal icing
- ★ piping bag with nos. 1.5 and 18 piping tubes
- ★ silver sugar balls: 4mm (¹/₅in), 6mm (³/₁₀in), 8mm (²/₅in)
- ★ white vegetable fat
- ★ edible white hologram dust

Add 2.5ml (½ tsp) glycerine to the icing to prevent it setting too hard.

1 Preheat the oven to 170°C/325°F/Gas Mark 3. Place the dry ingredients in a mixing bowl, add the butter and rub together with your fingertips until the mixture resembles fine breadcrumbs.

2 Make a hollow in the centre and pour in the beaten egg, golden syrup and vanilla extract. Mix together well, until you have a ball of dough. Place the dough in a plastic bag and chill in the fridge for 30 minutes.

3 Roll the dough out on a lightly floured surface to 5mm (⅕in) thick. Cut out snowflake shapes using the cutters and the no. 18 piping tube, removing geometric shapes from inside each snowflake.

4 Remove a small circle of dough from the top of the cookies using a piping tube. Lightly knead and re-roll the trimmings together to use up all the dough.

5 Place the cookies on greased baking sheets and bake for 12–15 minutes until lightly coloured and firm but not crisp. Leave on the tray for 2 minutes before transferring to a wire rack to cool.

6 Fill a piping bag fitted with a 1.5 tube with royal icing. Pipe lines and dots over the cookies and secure silver balls in place with a dot of royal icing.

7 Once the icing has dried, paint white vegetable fat over all the decoration and sprinkle with white hologram dust. Tie silver cord, ribbon or elastic to a selection of your snowflake cookies and hang as desired.

make royal icing ...

you will need ...
★ 1 egg white
★ 250g (9oz) icing (confectioners')
  sugar, sifted

1 Beat the egg white in a bowl until foamy. Gradually beat in the icing sugar until the icing is glossy and forms soft peaks.

2 The icing should have soft peak consistency, so adjust as necessary, adding either a little icing sugar or water as required. If you are not using the icing immediately, cover it with plastic wrap until you are ready for it.

beaded snowflakes

People say that no two snowflakes are alike, but how do they know? Apart from a change of colourway these pretty decorations are all the same, but you could make each one slightly different so that children or guests can have fun spotting the difference! To catch the light and add more festive sparkle you can fit silver-plated filagree caps at both ends of the pearls.

The main decoration is made with seed beads and fine silver-plated wire, with a crystal added in the centre to finish.

you will need ... (for one decoration)

★ 15cm (6in) snowflake wire

★ round pearls: twelve 6mm,
  six 8mm and six 10mm
  aquamarine round crystals:
  seven 6mm, six 8mm
  and six 10mm

★ round grooved metal beads:
  six 8mm and six 10mm

★ seed beads size 9 (2.5mm),
  15g colour-lined or silver-lined

★ filigree caps: twelve 7mm
  and twelve 10mm

★ bead glue

★ 0.315mm (30swg)
  silver-plated wire

Check that the beads you are using have a large enough hole to feed through a double length of wire easily.

1 On one stem of the snowflake wire pick up a 6mm crystal, 6mm pearl, 8mm grooved bead, 7mm filigree cap, 8mm pearl, 7mm filigree cap, 10mm pearl, 10mm grooved bead, 10mm filigree cap, 10mm pearl, 10mm filigree cap and an 8mm crystal. Apply glue to the end of the wire stem and then push on the final 6mm pearl (**a**).

a

2 Miss a stem then repeat the sequence on the next stem. Fill a third stem in the same way. To fill two other stems pick up a 6mm pearl, 8mm crystal, 10mm grooved bead, 10mm filigree cap, 10mm pearl, 10mm filigree cap, 10mm crystal, 8mm grooved bead, 7mm filigree cap, 8mm pearl, 7mm filigree cap, 6mm pearl and then stick a 6mm pearl at the end.

3 On the last stem feed half the beads on to the snowflake form. Fold a 20cm (8in) length of fine silver-plated wire in half and add the rest of the bead sequence on to it beginning with the small pearl. Apply glue on the end of the last stem and feed the beaded wire on to it. Pull the fine wire ends and beads until there is a short loop at the end and the beads are all on the snowflake form, and trim **(b)**.

4 To make the seed bead embellishment, cut a 36cm (14in) length of wire and twist a small loop on one end. Pick up 25 beads and drop them down until they are about 5cm (2in) from the loop. Holding the long wire tail, miss the end bead and feed the wire through the next three beads **(c)**. Pick up four beads and let them drop down to the stem. Miss the end bead and feed through the next three beads – this makes the first branch.

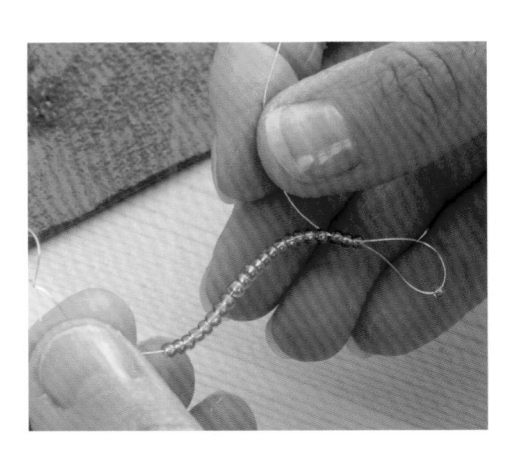

5 Feed the wire down through the next four beads on the stem and make two six-bead branches **(d)**. Feed the wire through the next six beads on the stem and make two eight-bead branches. Feed the wire through the last beads on the stem. Make six long snowflake stems in total.

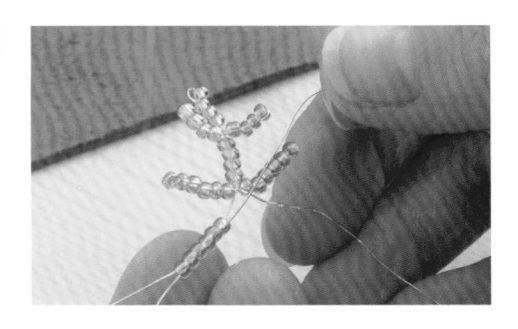

6 Wrap the wire ends around each stem near the centre of the snowflake (**e**). Make six shorter snowflake stems for the centre by picking up 14 seed beads to begin and then repeating the first part of the larger snowflake stem until there are two six-bead branches. Take the tail wire through the remaining beads to complete. Feed the wires of these snowflake stems into the centre of the snowflake decoration and twist all the wires together on the reverse side to secure.

f

e

7 Trim the wires neatly and push the end flat against the decoration. Finally, feed a 6mm crystal on to a length of fine wire. Tie it across the centre of the snowflake decoration (**f**), twist the wires together at the back and trim neatly.

Pre-formed snowflake wires are available in a range of sizes so you can choose the size to suit your Christmas tree, perhaps a large snowflake for the top and smaller decorations for hanging.

icicle droplets

These simple decorations can be made in next to no time and provide stylish, sparkling Christmas tree ornaments. An ideal project if you are short of time or just want to vary the shape and style of the decorations, so that each droplet is unique. Simply cut 15cm (6in) of 0.8mm (21swg) silver-plated wire and make a loop at one end. Coil the end round by hand to make a 1.5cm (⅝in) circle. Bend the tail at a right angle next to the coil. Add the beads, beginning with the largest and finishing with the smallest, applying beading glue before threading the last bead.

luxury stocking

Who says Christmas stockings are just for kids? The white silk velvet, silver-lined seed beads and crystals give this stocking an elegant frosty look. Indulge yourself or a friend and get ready for Santa by making this luxury devoré stocking to hang as a decoration from the mantelpiece or at the end of the bed – if you're really lucky it will be full of gifts on Christmas morning!

The stocking is made from silk velvet, which can be dyed any colour you like. You could also personalize the design by adding a name or favourite motif.

- ★ Fibre Etch™
- ★ 56 x 38cm (22 x 15in) silk velvet
- ★ beading needle: size 10
- ★ seed beads: size 9 (2.5mm),
- ★ 15g silver-lined clear
- ★ 200 5mm bicone crystals (polished beads)
- ★ 300 2.5mm silver ball beads
- ★ 25cm (10in) bead loom
- ★ 75 x 38cm (29½ x 15in) satin lining
- ★ 56 x 38cm (22 x 15in)
- ★ thin wadding
- ★ white sewing thread
- ★ silver machine embroidery thread
- ★ short length of cord

1 Pin the template to the reverse side of a piece of silk velvet and draw around with a pencil. Trace a star on to thin card and cut out. Draw around the card star four times on to the stocking shape. Following the manufacturer's guidelines, apply the Fibre Etch on to the star shapes. Keep within the lines and ensure each star is completely wetted with Fibre Etch. Dry with a hair dryer.

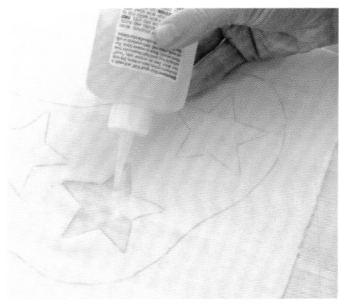

2 Press the reverse side of the stocking shape with a medium dry iron until the star shapes start to turn brown. Keep checking until the colour changes and the fabric feels brittle. Rinse out under a cold running tap, rubbing the pile away with your fingers. Hang until almost dry, then press on the reverse side.

3 Lay the velvet stocking shape on to a piece of lining fabric and then on to thin wadding. Pin the template in position and tack around the edge. Trim to 2cm (¾in) from the tacked line. For the back, cut another velvet stocking shape but facing the opposite direction. Lay on to thin wadding only and tack the outline as before and trim.

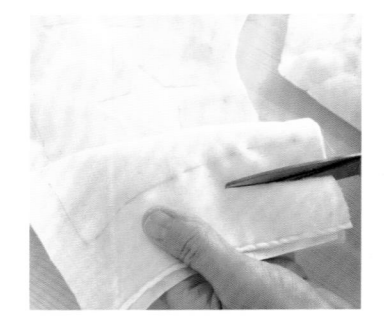

couching ...

Secure a double thread on the reverse side and bring the needle out at the end of one line. Pick up enough beads to fill the line and take the needle back through at the other end. Bring the needle back between each bead on one side of the laid thread and take back on the other side so that each bead is caught down on the fabric.

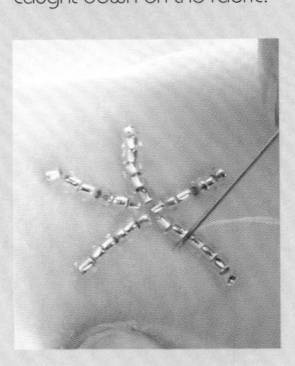

4 Secure a double length of sewing thread on the reverse side of the stocking panel and bring out between the stars. Pick up six silver-lined seed beads and take the needle back through to form a straight line. Couch over the centre beads. Repeat five more times to make a simple star shape and then sew a silver ball bead in the middle.

5 Bring a double thread out at the point of an etched star, pick up a silver ball bead and four silver-lined seed beads twice, then a final silver ball bead. Take the needle back through and couch over the bead strand. Repeat the process on each side of the star and for each of the stars.

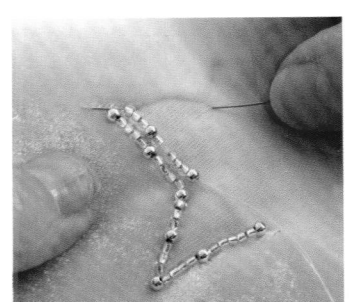

6 Fold the lining fabric with right sides together and cut two stocking shapes using the template and adding a 2cm (¾in) seam allowance. Pin a lining stocking with right sides together to each of the prepared velvet stocking panels. Sew along the top straight edge, trim to 6mm (¼in) and press open.

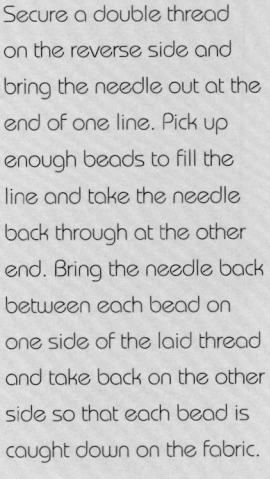

7 Pin the two stocking shapes with right sides together and sew around the tacked outline leaving a gap for turning through on one of the straight edges of the lining. Trim the seams and snip into any inward-facing curves. Notch the outward curves and turn the stocking through to the right side. Slipstitch the gap and tuck the lining inside the stocking. Ease out the curves and press from the reverse side.

8 To make the bead loom border, cut nine double lengths of silver thread and secure at one end of the bead loom. Using a beading needle, pick up 24 silver ball beads on to each pair of threads. Space out the pairs across the top of the bead loom so there are 6mm (¼in) gaps between the threads. Space in the same way across the bottom of the loom and secure.

9 Secure a double length of silver thread on one side at the top of the warp threads and above the silver ball beads. Using a long beading needle, * pick up eight bicone crystals and bring up below the warp threads. Take the thread back through all the beads above the warp threads. Bring a silver ball bead up close to the crystals on each thread. Take the needle through the first silver ball bead, then pick up eight crystals again. Repeat from * until all the crystals are used.

10 Pin the bead loom border panel to the front of the stocking. Oversew along the top and bottom edges to secure and sew in the warp thread ends of the panel at each side. Attach a cord or fabric loop to the inside of the stocking to hang.

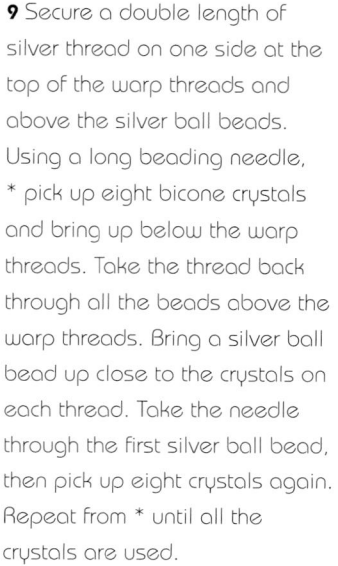

To prevent beads falling off in use, and for extra strength, always use a double thread to attach beads and secure on the reverse side with a double backstitch.

elf stocking

Make the stocking from two layers of purple felt and pin with a star in each of the other felt colours. Couch matching coloured seed beads around the stars adding additional single beads at each point and in the centre. Add coloured felt triangles around the stocking top and couch beads along the line. Make bell clusters by adding to jump rings and feed each through the central seed bead on each stars. Add a third jump ring to four of the clusters and sew to the back of the felt triangles. Finally, add a loop of ribbon for hanging and a few bells to the back edge.

Why not try this stocking which is quicker to make as there is no lining. You can use the frosty white colours used for the luxury stocking on page 42 or use brighter shades as shown here.

techniques basic sewing kit p. 88 ... overstitch p. 101 ... backstitch p. 103 ... slipstitch p. 100 ... working with beads p. 108 ... using a bead loom p. 109 **templates** p. 114

snowfall bag

Instead of a stocking, why not create a present sack decorated with festive trimmings? This stylish winter-themed gift bag features a cool colour scheme with snowflake motifs and looks even better when overflowing with Christmas presents!

you will need ...

★ 30 x 4cm
   (12 x 1½in)
★ turquoise wool
   felt fabric
★ 70 x 50cm
   (27½ x 20in)
★ pale lilac wool
   felt fabric
★ scraps of aqua
   and green wool
   felt fabric
★ 0.5m (½yd)
   lining fabric
★ white, blue and
   green six-stranded
   embroidery cotton
★ green and blue
   seed beads
★ 10 blue
   crystal beads
   fabric glue
★ snowflake
   templates
   (see page 114)

1 Cut the front and back panels from pale lilac felt, the sides and base from turquoise felt and the handles, loop and core fastening from aqua and green felts. Follow the instructions on pages 97–98 to make up the bag and lining.

2 Cut out motifs from the coloured felt scraps. Then layer, embroider with backstitch and embellish with beads.

3 Arrange the motifs and glue in place on the bag front.

A clever clasp, made from felt strips, provides an additional novelty feature.

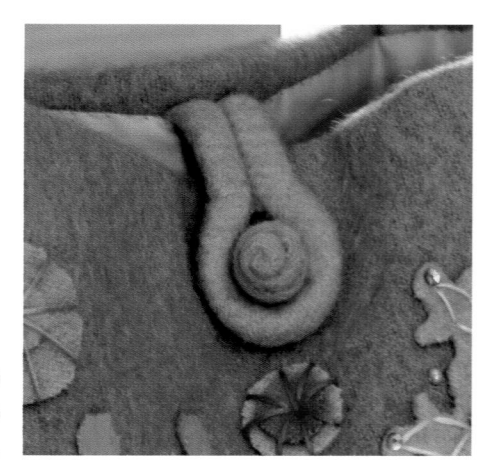

cute cupcakes

Cupcakes are without doubt 'a cake for all seasons' — and everyone will love these stylish seasonal cupcake designs. You can top them with icing or frosting and decorate with a range of sprinkles, colourings, sweets and decorations. Why not indulge yourself by swapping the vanilla extract for 50g of cocoa powder to make delicious chocolate cupcakes?

For an even finish when applying fondant icing, smooth it with a flat bladed knife that has been wetted and excess water shaken off.

you will need ...

for the vanilla cupcakes ...

★ 225g (8oz) slightly salted butter

★ 225g (8oz) caster sugar

★ 4 medium eggs

★ 225 (8oz) self-raising flour

★ 5ml (1 teaspoon) natural vanilla extract

for decorating ...

★ white fondant icing
  (see page 54)

★ rolled blue petal paste
  (see page 56)

★ reindeer and snowflake cutters

★ silver edible beads

The different sizes of baking cases and trays detailed here are:
- **Very Little** *petit four cases (1⅛in x 1in)*
- **Little** *31 x 23mm mini muffin cases*
- **Not So Little** *45 x 27mm (1¾ x 1¹/₁₆in) fairy cake cases*
- **Not At All Little** *muffin cases*

first frost

1 Pre-heat the oven to 175°C (347°F/Gas Mark 4). Place cases in bun trays.

2 Put sugar, sieved flour, chopped up butter and vanilla extract into a food processor. Blitz all together on medium power until well mixed. Alternatively mix it all together with a hand-held whisk.

3 Then add eggs one by one, using a slow pulse setting, if using a food processor, until the mix is integrated.

4 Spoon the mixture into the cases (so they are about half full, allowing room for your cakes to rise), and place in the baking tray. Place in the centre of the oven and bake for: 11–12 minutes (Very Little), 13–14 minutes (Little), 15–17 minutes (Not So Little) and 18–20 minutes (Not At All Little), or until the tops of the cakes spring back when lightly touched.

5 Turn out and cool on wire racks.

6 Carefully cover each cake with white fondant icing. Take a little extra time to ensure a crisp, clean finish around the edge.

7 For the snowflakes and reindeer, press your shapes from rolled blue petal paste. Use a cocktail stick to remove the shapes intact from their cutters.

8 Once dry, place them onto the cakes. If necessary, use a drop of watery icing sugar to help them bond. Gently press a silver bead into the centre of the star.

The vanilla sponge recipe should make one batch of: 48 Very Little cupcakes, 36 Little, 24 Not So Little or 12 Not At All Little cupcakes.

Christmas morning

Let your imagination run wild creating these simple but stylish designs! Cover each cake with white fondant icing and decorate with royal icing by piping festive designs on top. Try piping holly leaves, stars, presents, snowflakes and Christmas trees.

you will need ...

★ vanilla cupcakes
  (see page 52)

★ fondant icing

★ royal icing
  (see page 35)

★ green and red
  food colouring

★ fine-nozzled
  piping bag

★ yellow star
  decorations

This recipe is for pouring fondant but you can make ready-to-roll fondant by adding a greater quantity of icing sugar and kneading into a paste.

make fondant icing ...

you will need ...

★ 225g (8oz) sifted icing sugar

★ 2-3 tablespoons liquid glucose

★ white of 1 medium egg

1 Follow the method for royal icing on page 35, adding the liquid glucose to the mixture. You will need a spreading consistency, but not too thin as it will run too fast to the edges of the cupcake.

2 Cover with a clean cloth and leave for 30 minutes before using.

perfect present

These mini cupcakes make great Christmas treats and are so quick and simple to make. Simply ice your cakes with fondant icing and decorate with petal paste shapes, adding edible glue and a sprinkling of edible glitter. Then arrange into boxes padded with tissue paper.

you will need ...

- ★ vanilla cupcakes (see page 52)
- ★ fondant icing (see page 54)
- ★ small quantity of
- ★ petal paste
- ★ several colourings
- ★ cutters for bells,
- ★ stars, baubles and holly leaves
- ★ small cake boxes (about 10 x 10 x 6cm), preferably with a window lid
- ★ tissue paper

Colouring for icing is available in various forms, such as liquid and paste. Use a cocktail stick to add a little colouring at a time to ensure you get the perfect shade.

make petal paste ...

you will need ...

- ★ 225g (8oz) sifted icing sugar
- ★ 10–15ml (2–3 tablespoons) liquid glucose
- ★ 15ml (1 tablespoon) powdered gelatine
- ★ 5ml (1 teaspoon) glycerine
- ★ 1 egg white

1 Follow the method for royal icing on page 35, including the additional ingredients, then knead on a board dusted with cornflour for 10 minutes.

2 Add more icing sugar if necessary to get a dough consistency.

Noel bunting

Christmas is a special time to make the house warm, cosy and festive by adding trimmings and embellishments. This fun and colourful bunting is easy to make and not only looks fantastic but should last for many years to come. It can also be adapted to include different lettering and motifs.

This bunting uses a warm and festive colour theme and features a range of cute motifs created from different felts, ribbons, buttons and embroidery stitches.

you will need ...

★ two fat quarters of co-ordinating fabric (or lots of scraps)

★ 0.25m (¼yd) thin cotton wadding

★ 2m (2yd) of 7.6cm (3in) wide binding

★ 5.5m (6yd) wide and 40.6cm (16in) narrow ric-rac braid

★ fat eighth of fabric for lettering

★ fat eighth of fusible webbing

★ 25.4 x 25.4cm (10 x 10in) cream, green, golden and brown wool/mix felt for decorations each

★ decorative buttons: two star buttons for top of tree, ten small black buttons for gingerbread man and snowmen eyes, ten small heart buttons for gingerbread man and snowmen, four small white buttons for mistletoe

making the flags ...

1 Trace the template and cut out eight flags from the main fabric (different fabrics or all the same – see tip). Cut another eight flags from the lining fabric, and then eight from the thin cotton wadding, but make them 1.3cm (½in) bigger all the way around.

2 Using the templates, blanket stitch appliqué the letters NOEL on four of the flags. On the other four flags appliqué two mistletoe motifs and two Christmas trees. Note: the tree branches are added later in ric-rac but are given in the template to allow you to make them from fabric if you prefer. Don't add any trimmings and finery as these will come later.

3 Cut eight pieces of wide ric-rac 40.6cm (16in) long. Sew to the right side of the main flags. Make sure the edge of the ric-rac lines up with the edge of the bunting. Do not sew along the top edge. When you come to sew around the bottom of the bunting, gently ease around the curve.

4 With the wrong side of the flag facing you, place it on top of the lining, right sides together and place both of these on top of the cotton wadding. Centralize the bunting, pin well and sew, using the line of stitching you used to sew the ric-rac on, as a guide. Sew all the way around but not along the top edge. Trim your seams to a scant 6mm (¼in) – this may mean cutting off some of the ric-rac but it is necessary. Turn the flags the right way out, press well and trim the top edge. Top stitch 6mm (¼in) in from the edge of the bunting either by hand or machine.

5 Cut a length of binding 7.6cm (3in) wide x 2m (2yd) long. Cut a length of ric-rac 2m (2yd) long. Leave the first 15.2cm (6in) free then sew the ric-rac to the top of the flags as before. You should have a rough 15.2cm (6in) overhang on each end. Lay the binding right side to the flags and sew it on with a 6mm (¼in) seam, or one that is appropriate to the ric-rac. Sew the binding on to the ric-rac at the beginning and end. Press, turn over and slipstitch in place. Turn under the ends of the ric-rac for a neat finish. Decorate the mistletoe and Christmas tree with ric-rac and buttons.

To make the most economical use of the fat quarter, cut the flags one the right way and the next upside down and so on.

making the decorations ...

6 Stars: Mark or iron the freezer paper template on to felt. Do not cut. Stitch around the outside of the shape. Trim to a scant 6mm (¼in). Cut a slit in the middle of one side and turn right way out. Stuff very gently and then close the slit with ladder stitch. Blanket stitch all the way around the outside edge and stitch a button in the centre

7 Gingerbread, Holly and Snowmen: Make these in the same way as the stars using the relevant templates. To decorate the gingerbread man, stitch around the shape with two strands of red embroidery thread. Sew on three red heart buttons. Use two small buttons for eyes and draw or embroider the face. Cut out eight holly leaves from felt and blanket stitch them together in pairs using two strands of red thread. Backstitch the leaf veins in red. Sew the holly leaves to the bunting using red buttons for berries. For the snowman, sew on the eyes and heart buttons and embroider an orange nose. Tie ribbon around his neck. Sew the decorations to the binding to finish.

Bunting is easy to adapt to other celebrations such as birthdays and weddings by using appropriate colours, fabrics and embellishments.

techniques basic equipment p. 88 ... blanket stitch p. 102 ... slipstitch p. 99 ... ladder stitch p. 100 ... backstitch p. 101 ...
topstitch p. 95 ... sewing on buttons p. 109   *templates* pp. 114–115

clever cards

Stitching with a sewing machine is an incredibly easy way to create unique Christmas cards. A simple zigzag stitch in a bright sewing thread makes a bold statement and adds textural interest, while holding layers of card together. Here strips of red card are machine stitched onto white linen-effect card to create a stylish and contemporary Christmas tree design.

If making several cards at the same time, why not vary the design slightly by changing the colour of the card or threads. A green or silvery white colour theme would work equally well here.

you will need ...

★ 13 x 10cm (5 x 4in)
   red card

★ 11.5 x 11.5cm
   (4½ x 4½in) white
   linen-effect card

★ 13 x 13cm (5 x 5in)
   red single-fold card

★ sewing machine

★ white sewing thread

★ sewing needle

★ star punch

trim the trees

1 Using a metal ruler, craft knife and cutting mat, cut strips from the red card 1cm (³⁄₈in) wide and 13cm (5in) long.

2 Cut the strips into five lengths of 9.5cm, 8cm, 6cm, 4cm and 2.5cm (3¾in, 3⅛in, 2³⁄₈in, 1½in and 1in) and use a glue stick to attach each piece to the white card square.

3 Machine sew a zigzag stitch along the centre of the longest strip. Remove from the machine and trim either end of the thread to 10cm (4in). Repeat with the remaining strips.

4 Thread each loose end onto the needle. Take through to the reverse side of the card, pulling the thread all the way through and remove from the needle.

5 Turn the card over and place two lengths of adhesive tape over the thread ends to make sure they don't unravel and trim the excess.

6 Place double-sided adhesive tape along each edge on the reserve of the white card. Peel off the backing of each tape piece halfway and fold outwards. Position the card over the red single-fold card and remove all the tape backing.

7 Punch a star and cut a tree base 1.3 x 1cm (½ x ⅜in) from red card and glue both on the white card.

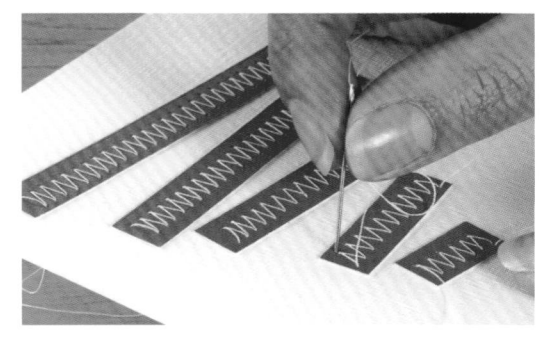

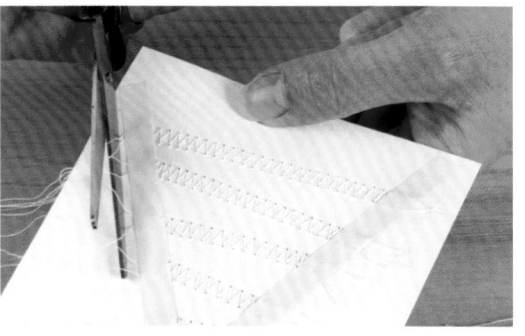

Make a matching tag by cutting a simple tree shape from white card and machine sewing to a red card triangle with red running stitch. The thread ends should be taken through and covered by a second red card triangle glued to the reverse and a hole punched through the top with a ribbon threaded through and tied in a bow.

techniques basic sewing kit p. 88 ... using a sewing machine p. 93 ... zigzag stitch p. 95

all wrapped up

A card that resembles a gift is guaranteed to grab attention! This variation is easily achieved using colourful card and shiny ribbon with a flamboyant bow. The choices of colour schemes, papers and ribbons are endless, giving you the opportunity to indulge your imagination.

you will need ...

★ 20 x 30cm (8 x 12in) red card

★ 10 x 10cm (4 x 4in) pink and orange card

★ 1m (1yd) length of gold ribbon

★ circle punches: 1.5cm (³⁄₈in) and 1cm (³⁄₈in)

1 Using the template on page 116, cut out the card, score the spine and slit the spine to accommodate the ribbon width.

2 Punch 11 larger pink and 11 smaller orange circles and glue to the front of the card with PVA glue.

3 Thread the ribbon through the spine, cross at the back and tie a bow at the top. Trim the ribbon ends diagonally.

Don't forget to colour coordinate the envelope with the card.

Punched circles have been used to create a spotty giftwrap design. Try using strips of different coloured papers to create a stripy pattern.

sparkling stars

Bring an extra sparkle to the festive season with the clever use of sequins. By threading star-shaped sequins onto metallic thread and allowing them to hang, they create a dazzling display as they turn and twinkle.

you will need ...

★ 14.5 x 14.5cm (5¾ x 5¾ in) green single-fold card

★ 15 x 13cm (6 x 5in) silver card

★ 10 x 10cm (4 x 4in) green card

★ 13 x 13cm (5 x 5in) bright pink felt

★ about 23 x 1cm (³⁄₈in) wide silver sequin stars

★ silver star outline peel-off stickers

★ silver metallic sewing thread

★ sewing needle

1 Glue the pink felt to the green folded card and attach five strips of the silver card. Knot the sequins onto the silver threads, insert the threads through the top of the felt and card and secure on the reverse with a peel-off stickers.

2 Using the templates on page 116, cut out stars from green and silver card and glue to the felt.

Try using different sequins and colour combinations. You could also use card instead of the pink felt.

stylish table settings

There is something very special about Christmas decorations that are handmade. This cheerful runner is inspired by the traditional Scherenschnitte paper cuts of Switzerland and Germany. With its simplistic folk art motifs, it's sure to be the centrepiece of your Christmas table and a treasured heirloom for years to come.

The red and white colour combination is typically Scandinavian and suits the Christmas theme, but you could use green and white or any other festive colours that suit your room.

you will need ...

★ roll of red Kraft paper

★ roll of white Kraft paper

★ small paintbrush for applying glue

★ swivel knife, such as a Coluzzle knife, and cutting mat, if required

★ rubber roller

★ PVA glue

★ sticky putty, such as Blu-Tack

★ metal ruler

★ templates (see pages 117–119)

If you can't get hold of a rubber roller, simply press down firmly with your thumbs, working from the centre of each element out towards the edges.

1 Cut a piece of red paper 40cm (16in) wide and as long as you require plus a piece of white backing paper to the same size plus 10cm (4in) all round.

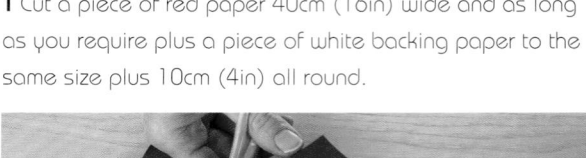
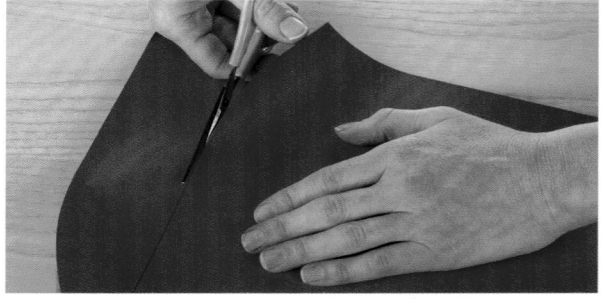

2 Trace all the runner templates and place face down on the back of the runner and redraw over the lines to transfer the images. You can repeat some of the images, for example the trees and snowman, to fill the space as necessary.

3 Shade in all the areas of the design that you wish to keep (or remove) before you start to avoid cutting away the wrong parts.

4 Using a cutting mat and working on the main panel first, cut out the small details, such as the roof tiles and tree decorations first. Once the details are completed, cut away the paper from around the main parts of the design.

5 Cut carefully around the stockings, stars, holly and bauble in the border at the top of the runner, making sure they stay attached. A swivel knife makes this easier.

6 Slide the runner onto the length of white backing paper. Place centrally and make sure the design is flat and not distorted. Attach the corners of the runner to the paper with sticky putty such as Blu-Tack.

7 Lift one section of the paper cut at a time and apply PVA glue to the back with a small brush.

8 Drop the paper cut down onto the backing paper and pat gently into place using your fingertips. Take care not to wrinkle the paper cut or stretch it out of shape.

9 Once the paper cut is glued in position, carefully go over it with a rubber roller to bond it to the backing paper and remove any air bubbles.

10 When the glue is dry, trim away the excess white paper with a craft knife and metal ruler.

Christmas cheer

If you don't have time for a large project like the festive table runner, adapt the idea to create a set of coasters. Trace the images you like and make them in the same way as the runner. You'll still have some Scandinavian Christmas style but in a fraction of the time.

Use the smaller designs from the runner, such as the baubles, holly leaves, stockings and presents, to make these simple coasters. Or if you're good at drawing, you could even create your own motifs.

snowflake tea lights

you will need ...

★ glass tea light holders

★ scraps of white and pale blue tissue paper

★ zigzag scissors

★ spray glue

★ self-adhesive clear glass stones

These tea lights are decorated with elegant, fine-lined paper snowflakes. Tissue paper is used as it is thin enough to lie smoothly against the outside of the glass. Because of its translucency, when the candlelight shines through it illuminates the colour, giving the illusion of stained glass.

1 Using zigzag scissors, cut thin strips of tissue paper and glue these around the rim and base of the tea light holders.

2 Trace the snowflake templates on page 111 onto a folded circle of tissue paper and glue into position on the tea light holders. Attach clear glass stones to the centre and tips of each snowflake.

The tissue-paper snowflakes can be attached to windows with a little spray glue. Or you could trace the templates onto card to create tree decorations.

For added sparkle, you could decorate the tissue paper snowflakes with glitter glue or silver sequins.

glittering baubles

Baubles are a Christmas essential but these exquisitely beaded ornaments are so gorgeous you won't want to put them away with the rest of the decorations. Each is made from the same basic beaded net, which is worked flat on a surface, with five bead colours that match the colour of the bauble. The finished baubles delightfully catch the light and will add glitter and elegance to any Christmas tree or window.

These beaded baubles use three different beading techniques: fringing, netting and tassels.

you will need ...

★ **15g size 8 beads**
(Rayher beads in
transparent purple,
silver-lined purple,
porcelain purple,
alabaster purple
and purple hex)

★ **15cm (6in) of 0.3mm**
(30swg) silver-plated wire

★ white quilting thread

★ size 10 long and short
beading needles

★ embroidery scissors

★ craft scissors

*Use a short beading needle
to work the netting and a long
beading needle to work the
fringing on the baubles.*

1 Cut a 30cm (12in) length of
wire and pick up the following
sequence of beads: silver-lined,
alabaster, transparent and
porcelain – referred to for the
rest of the project as (s,a,t,p).
If you have different beads,
arrange them in order and
label them to make it easier to
follow the pattern. Repeat the
sequence five times so there are
24 beads on the wire. Feed one
end of the wire through all the
beads again, pull tight, twist the
ends together and trim.

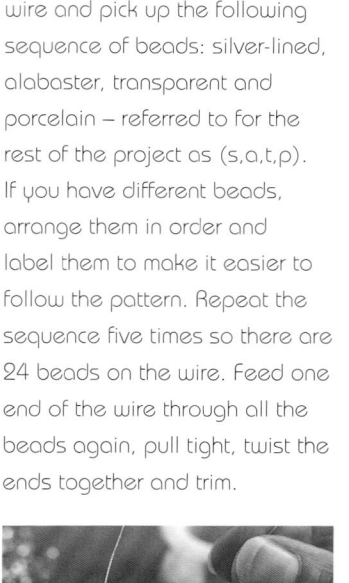

2 Cut six 1m (39½in) lengths of
white quilting thread and feed
one through each alabaster
bead, pulling halfway through
so all the ends are at the same
level. Thread a beading needle
on to one of the thread ends and
pick up a hex, silver-lined bead,
a hex, then an alabaster bead.

3 Thread a needle on the next thread along (not the other end of the previous thread). Pick up a hex, a silver-lined bead and a hex. Take the needle through the last bead from the previous thread to create the first point of a star. Repeat until all the threads are beaded and there are six points in a star shape.

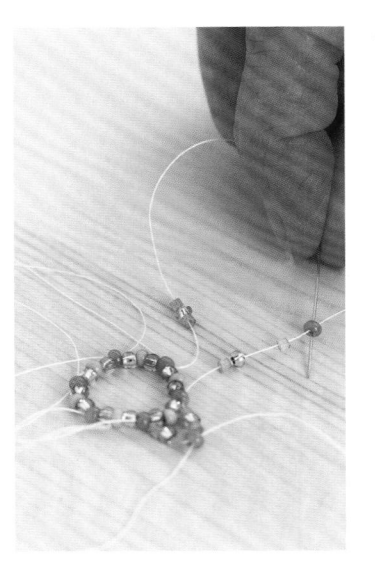

4 On the second round, pick up seven beads on the first thread: hex, (s,a,t,p), hex and silver-lined. On the next thread round, pick up the first six beads in the same order as before. Take the thread back through the last silver-lined bead. Repeat all the way round. On the third round, pick up 11 beads on one thread (hex, (s,a,t,p), (s,a,t,p), hex and alabaster) and thread the first 10 on the next thread. Complete in the same way as the previous round.

5 At this stage you should have a large star shape with six points. This time, working with a pair of threads from one point, pick up eight alabaster beads on the left-hand thread. Go back through the first four beads again with the same thread. Take the other thread through the second four beads. Feed both threads through an alabaster bead. On the next point repeat with silver-lined beads and finish with an alabaster bead at the bottom. Alternate these loops all the way round.

6 Working with one thread from adjacent points again, begin to reverse the shaping. Pick up a hex (s,a,t,p), (s,a,t,p), hex and alabaster. On the next thread pick up the first nine beads and take the needle through the last alabaster in the same direction so the hole is vertical. Repeat all the way round.

7 Working with the pairs of thread from the alabaster beads, pick up six beads on each thread: hex, (s,a,t,p) and hex. At this stage it is a good idea to check the fit over the bauble and alter the number of beads just added so they will fit into another beaded wire ring.

8 Make a wire ring as in step 1. Take one thread end through an alabaster bead, secure with a double half hitch and feed the thread around the ring to the next alabaster bead. Take the other thread end from the pair and feed through the next alabaster bead, secure with a half hitch and again feed through to the next alabaster bead. Repeat so there are three adjacent pairs of threads secured.

double half hitch

Use this knot to secure a thread in netting or fringes before feeding the end through several more beads and trimming the end.

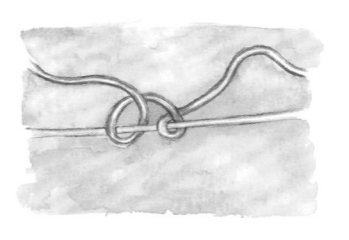

9 Slip the net over the bauble and secure the remaining three pairs of threads on the ring, so there are pairs of threads coming out either side of the six alabaster beads.

10 To make a fringe strand, use one thread and pick up a hex and (s,a,t,p) six times so there are 30 beads on the string. Pick up four silver-lined beads and feed the thread back up several beads. Work a half hitch to secure and feed the needle up several more beads, leaving a tail. Bring the next thread down through the bead string and feed through the four silver-lined beads again. Pick up two silver-lined beads, take the needle between the threads at the bottom of the previous four beads and pick up another two silver-lined beads. Finish the berry by taking the needle down through two beads, picking up two silver-lined beads and feeding the needle back through to the strand. Secure as before and trim ends. Make five more strands this way.

11 To fill the large net holes, feed a 50cm (20in) length of quilting thread through the top silver-lined bead in each net. Using both threads together, pick up a hex, (s,a,t,p), silver and alabaster. Make a loop with eight porcelain beads as step 5 and pull the loop tight. Make a second loop with eight transparent beads. Pick up (s,a,t,p), silver and alabaster and feed the threads through the alabaster bead at the bottom of the net hole. Secure threads. Repeat in each large net hole.

Once you've made the first bauble it is easy to vary the net pattern to create a more ornate net. Just begin with the star and then experiment, adding extra threads if required.

techniques

basic sewing kit

Each project in this book has its own You Will Need list, detailing the particular materials and equipment required to make it; however, the basic sewing kit details those additional items that you are most often likely to need as you work. Before you begin, do take the time to collect together the recommended items.

Measuring tools

• **Ruler (1)** for measuring or marking out and cutting against – ideally use a ruler with both metric and imperial conversions.

• **Tape measure (2)** Handy for measuring long lengths where a ruler is too short.

Adhesives

• **Fabric glue (3)** is quick and easy to use and is essential for attaching items that are too small or fiddly to stitch in place, or for sticking on ribbons and braids where you don't want to see stitching.

• **Fabric spray adhesive** is a useful product, as it temporarily places a fabric, thereby enabling you to move it around if necessary.

• **Double-sided tape (4)** will come in handy when you want to fix items temporarily.

• **Bondaweb**, a double-sided fusible webbing, comes in a roll or in pre-cut pieces. It looks like paper and is used to apply appliqué motifs and for joining pieces of fabric together permanently.

Scissors

• **Dressmaking shears (5)** for cutting out fabric.

• **Embroidery scissors (6)** have small sharp blades, ideal for fine work and intricate cutting.

• **General-purpose scissors** useful for cutting out patterns and general use.

• **Pinking shears** cut a zigzag edge that can be used to neaten seams or give a decorative edge.

Threads

• **Sewing thread (7)** is used for sewing patchwork and for project assembly by machine or hand. These are easy to cut and sew and don't fray too readily. For best results, use a thread that matches the fibre content of the fabric you are working with and that is the same colour or slightly darker in shade. For tasks that require strong thread, you'll find buttonhole thread or topstitching thread useful. General-purpose polyester sewing thread is ideal for machine sewing and hand-sewing and comes in a kaleidoscope of colours.

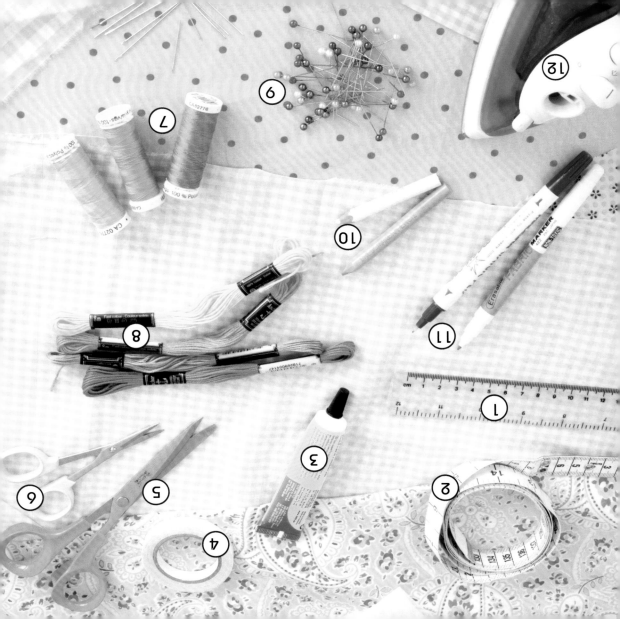

• **Embroidery threads (8)** are infinite in their colour, variety and finish; they include stranded embroidery cotton (floss) as shown in the photograph on page 89, soft cotton, coton perlé, coton à broder and metallic threads for hand or machine stitching.

Pins

• **General dressmakers' pins (9)** keep fabric pieces in place before sewing. The colourful glass heads are easy to see against the fabric.

• **Extra-fine bridal and lace pins** are required for pinning delicate fabrics.

• **Safety pins** come in useful for turning through channels or pinning fabrics together.

Marking tools

• **Fabric pencils (10)** or tailors' chalk can be used to draw a line or pattern. The marks rub off once the stitching is complete.

• **Fabric markers (11)** such as vanishing fade-away markers are ideal, as they disappear after several hours on their own, or with a little water, so won't leave a mark once the sewing is completed.

Pressing tools

• **Iron and ironing board (12)** – see tip below.

• **Pressing cloth** this needn't be expensive – just a large square of muslin that will help protect your fabric and your iron.

Sewing machine

You will need a reliable lockstitch sewing machine that can sew straight and zigzag stitches. Utility stitches and a small range of embroidery stitches are also useful. A sewing machine will produce much stronger seams than hand sewing and can be quicker and easier to use once you are familiar with it. See Using a Sewing Machine, page 93, for more information.

tip

When pressing, the iron is pressed lightly onto the fabric, lifted and moved onto the next area. It should not be confused with ironing, which is when the iron glides over the fabric surface. Pins and tacking stitches should be removed before pressing and the heat settings adjusted on the iron according to the fabric type.

preparing for work

Before you start to work on your selected project, there are a few things you will need to prepare in advance. You will need to get together any templates listed for the project, make a pattern if necessary, prepare your fabrics for work, and mark, pin and cut out any fabric pieces. This section outlines a few essential 'getting ready' techniques.

Preparing patterns

Details of any templates required are given in the techniques bar at the end of a project. The templates are located on pages 110–119. They need to be enlarged on a photocopier at the percentage given. If you need to make a paper template, you can pin it onto the fabric and then either cut it out around the template or use a fabric pen or pencil to draw around the template before cutting it out.

Pinning patterns

General dressmakers' pins are suitable for most fabrics, although silks and fine cotton should be pinned with bridal or lace pins. Pin the straight grain first, then pin around the pattern piece, diagonally at the corners and vertical to the pattern edge.

Marking fabrics

There are two ways to mark out designs onto your fabrics before stitching.

Using a fade-away pen

Any marks made with a fade-away pen will disappear on their own or with a little water. Use the pen to draw the line you want to follow with stitching. Once stitched, dab with a little water on your finger to remove any traces of the marks.

Using a fabric pencil or tailors' chalk

Any marks made with a fabric pencil or tailors' chalk will easily rub off once applied. Draw the line or pattern with the pencil or chalk and take care not to rub it out as you stitch. Once the stitching is complete, rub the marks to remove.

Preparing the fabric

Prepare your fabrics by pre-washing them before use in mild detergent to check that the colours do not run and to allow for any shrinkage that might occur. If you are using a cotton lining or interfacing, you should pre-wash this as well. For delicate fabrics such as silk and wool that cannot be washed, you can gently tighten the fibres by hovering a steam iron 3–4cm (1¼–1¾in) above the cloth. Once you have completed this process the fibres shouldn't shrink any further. If the fabrics lack body after washing, iron while damp with a little spray starch, but be careful – too much starch leaves white marks on dark fabrics.

Cutting the fabric

It is always important when cutting out to have a clean, large flat surface to work on. Cut with the grain of the fabric, or if you are working with printed stripes and checks, cut with the pattern for best results. Always cut away from yourself.

Using scissors

Ensure that your dressmaking shears are sharp. To cut accurately, position your fabric to the left of the shears (or to the right if you are left-handed) and follow the edge of the pattern line, taking long strokes for straight edges and shorter strokes for curved areas.

Using a rotary cutter

The rotary cutter has a very sharp blade and is perfect for cutting out fabric into strips or squares, for patchwork for example.

1 Position a ruler firmly on top of your fabric and square off any uneven ends.

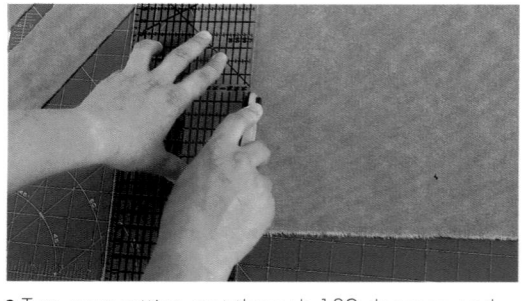

2 Turn your cutting mat through 180 degrees and line up the relevant mark on the ruler – e.g. 6.5cm (2½in) if 5cm (2in) is the finished size required (allowing for the seam allowance when sewing the fabric squares together). Line up your rotary cutter against the ruler's edge and cut.

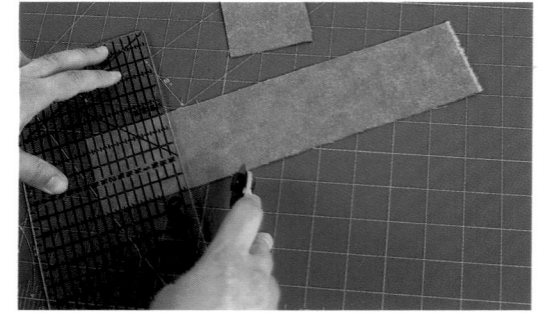

using a sewing machine

Although it is possible to make most of the projects in this book by hand stitching, the sewing machine will produce a more consistent and stronger stitch, and you will be able to complete projects so much faster. It is well worth the investment if you intend doing a lot of sewing.

Getting started with the sewing machine

Take some time to read your sewing machine manual and become familiar with the different parts before you begin.

> **tip** It is always a good idea to test stitch on a scrap of your chosen fabric before beginning a project.

Presser feet

The presser foot holds the fabric firmly against the needle plate while the stitch is formed. It is important to use the correct presser foot for the stitch you are using and to test your tension on a scrap of fabric before you begin. Here are a few presser feet that you will find useful:

• **General-purpose foot (a)** for general sewing, utility and embroidery stitches on ordinary fabrics.

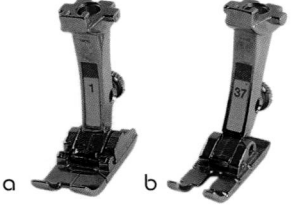

a   b

• **Clear view foot (b)** essential for accurate work as it allows you to see where you are stitching. It can be made from clear plastic or cut away. This is ideal for working on bulky fabrics and for machine appliqué.

Machine needles

Use an appropriate machine needle for your work and change it frequently – immediately if damaged or bent. Popular needle sizes are:

• **Size 70 (9)** for silks and fine cottons **(a)**.
• **Size 90 (14)** for denims, canvas and heavy weight linens **(b)**.

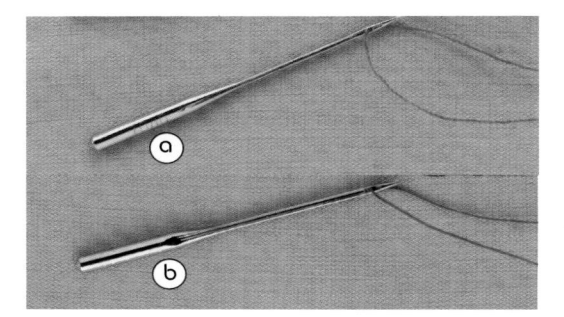

Preparing for machine sewing

Before you begin to stitch, it is worth taking the time to make sure your material is ready. Pinning and tacking (basting) are quick and useful ways of ensuring your fabric is lined up and stays in the correct place when machine sewing.

Tacking (basting)

Tacking (basting) fabrics together will ensure that they stay in place as you sew them. You can remove the stitches afterwards. Using a thin thread, sew the fabrics together with large running stitches. When you reach the end of the fabric, do not secure the thread with a knot.

Once the fabrics have been sewn together, use an unpicker tool or a pin to pull out the tacking stitches.

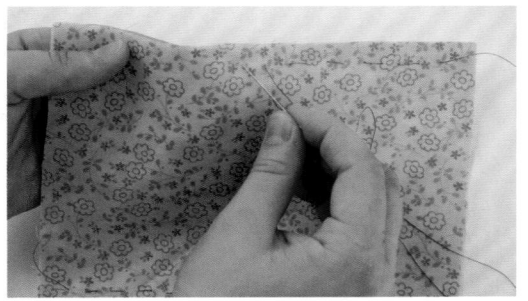

Pinning

To sew two fabrics together by machine without tacking (basting), use this quick and easy technique. Place your fabrics together, edge to edge. Insert the pins at right angles to the edges of the fabrics, leaving a small even gap between the pins.

Stitch slowly over the pins – the needle will slip over each pin without bending them – and then remove the pins once the stitching is complete.

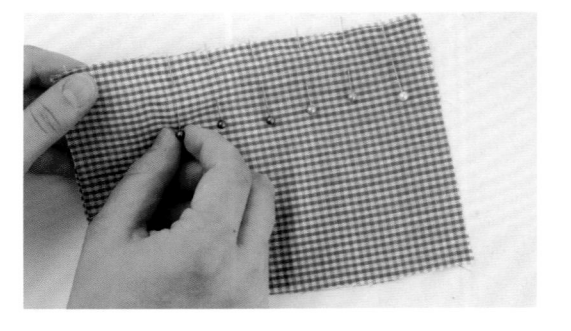

Machine stitches

The type of machine you have will determine the range of stitches available to you. Listed here are the main types of stitches that you will need to use on your sewing machine to complete the projects in this book.

Straight stitch (a)

All sewing machines will sew straight stitch and this is the type of stitch most widely used to join two pieces of fabric together. It can be used for sewing seams, topstitching and understitching. For ordinary fabric, set your stitch length to 3mm (⅛in) for tidy, even stitches. For fine fabrics use a shorter stitch length, and increase the stitch length for heavier fabrics.

tip If your stitches are different lengths, there may be a problem with your needle. Are you using the right needle for the fabric? Is the needle blunt and is it inserted properly?

Zigzag (b)

Zigzag is a versatile stitch, used to neaten seams and edges, as a decorative edge and to hold appliqué motifs in place. To neaten seams, it is best to set your zigzag stitch to 2mm (³⁄₃₂in) width and 2mm (³⁄₃₂in) length. When using for appliqué, set your zigzag to 2mm (³⁄₃₂in) and between 0.5 and 1mm (³⁄₃₂–¹⁄₁₆in) in length.

Understitching (c)

Understitching is used to keep facings and linings from rolling and becoming visible from the front. Trim back the seam allowances to 3mm (⅛in) and press to the side where the understitching is to be applied. Work a straight stitch from the right side and sew close to the pressed seam. The facing or lining can then be turned under and pressed and will lie flat.

Topstitching (d)

Topstitching is straight stitch set at about 3mm (⅛in) in length. It can be both decorative and functional, while holding the seam firmly in place. Place the presser foot onto the edge of the seam and use this as a guide to keep the stitching line straight.

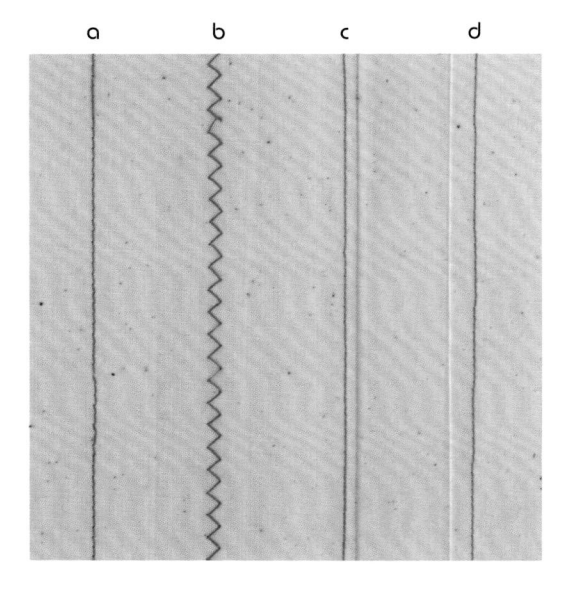

Satin stitch

Satin stitch is a zigzag stitch with the stitch length set at almost zero. It can be used to appliqué fabric patches, for buttonholes, and to provide a decorative effect. Check that the stitch width is right for the fabric before you start as satin stitch can sometimes make the fabric gather if the stitches are too wide. The faster you stitch, the more even your satin stitch will be.

Sewing by machine

The following basic techniques work to a 1.5cm (½in) seam allowance, which can be adjusted for each project as necessary.

Sewing a seam

1 Tack (baste) or pin the seam across the seam line, with the right sides of your fabric together.

2 Place your fabric under the presser foot so that the edge of the seam is next to the 1.5cm (½in) line on the needle plate and the fabric is 5mm (¼in) behind the needle. Use the hand wheel to take the needle down into the fabric, and then begin to sew.

3 Sew at a comfortable speed, guiding the fabric along the 1.5cm (½in) line on the needle plate.

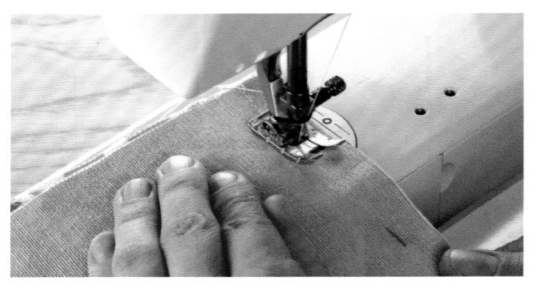

Neatening seams

Finished seams can be neatened in a number of different ways to prevent them from fraying and becoming weakened – machine zigzagging the raw edges is one of the fastest. Try different lengths and widths of the stitch to find which best suits the fabric. Generally, the stitch should be as small and narrow as possible. Trim the seam to 6mm (¼in) and zigzag both edges together.

Turning corners

1 Stitch down the first length, leaving a 1.5cm (½in) seam allowance. Slow down as you approach the corner and use the hand wheel to complete the last few stitches.

2 Stop 1.5cm (½in) from the edge of the fabric, with the needle in the fabric. Lift the presser foot and turn the fabric around until the next seam is lined up with the guideline on the needle plate. Lower the presser foot and continue to sew.

Sewing curves

A useful technique for stitching around curved corners or machine appliquéing shapes onto fabric.

• **For soft curves** Sew slowly, keeping the edge of the fabric opposite the presser foot on the guide-line of the needle plate.

• **For tighter curves** Stop and turn the fabric into the curve before beginning. Keep stopping every few stitches to adjust the line of the fabric until the curve is complete.

Making a bag

These step-by-step instructions will make the felt tote bag on page 48 but can be adapted for use with alternative materials, made to different dimensions and embellished with other designs and trimmings.

1 Measure and mark out two bag sides 36 x 7cm (14¼ x 2¾in) and a bag base 7 x 32cm (2¾ x 12½in) from one of the coloured felt fabrics, and the bag front and back 36 x 32cm (14½ x 12½in) from a different coloured fabric, then cut out.

2 With right sides facing, pin the bag front to one of the bag sides and machine stitch together, taking in a 6mm (¼in) seam allowance. Repeat for the bag back and remaining side. With right sides facing, pin the back and side to the front and side, plus the bag base to the bottom, and machine stitch as before.

3 Measure and mark out on the lining fabric two sides 28 x 7cm (15 x 2¾in), a base 7 x 32cm (2¾ x 12½in) and a front and back 38 x 32cm (15 x 12½in), then cut out. With right sides facing, pin and machine stitch the lining together, as for the bag.

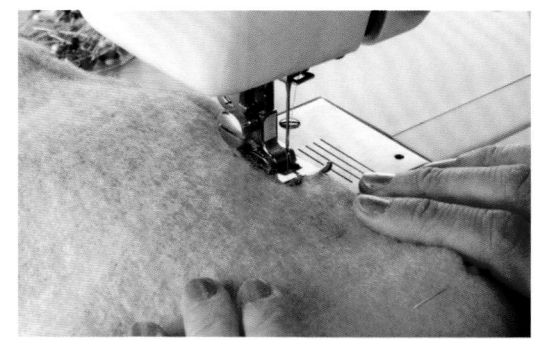

4 Cut two long strips 5 x 56cm (2 x 22in) from the coloured felt and roll up to form two long tubes. Pin, then slipstitch the open edge closed. Measure 6.5cm (2½in) from each side along the top edge of the front and back of the bag and hand stitch the handle ends in place.

5 Cut a 1.5 x 22cm (¾ x 8¾in) strip of coloured felt and roll it into a tube. Pin, then stitch the open edge closed. Form the tube into a loop and hand stitch the ends together for 8.5cm (3¼in). Hand stitch securely to the centre inside back edge of the bag.

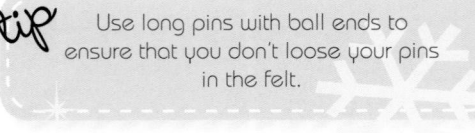
tip Use long pins with ball ends to ensure that you don't loose your pins in the felt.

6 Cut a 2 x 13cm (¾ x 5in) strip of coloured felt and roll it up to form a cone shape. Sew the end of the strip to the cone very securely to stop it unravelling. Sew the cone to the front of the bag in a corresponding position to the loop, so they form a fastening.

7 Turn over and press down a 2cm (¾in) hem around the top edge of the lining. Push the lining into the bag and pin it to the bag just below the top edge. Hand stitch in place using 'invisible' slipstitches.

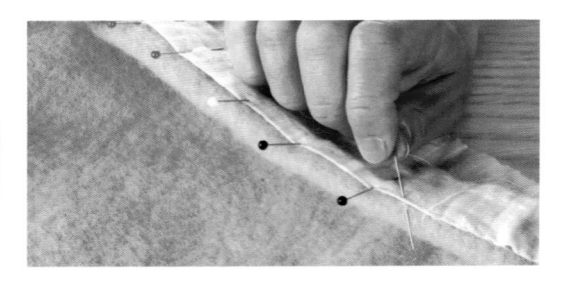

sewing by hand

The projects in this book use a variety of hand stitches for functional and decorative work, however they are all basic stitches that are easy to work simply by following the step-by-step photographs and diagrams given.

Hand-sewing needles

Choose a needle that matches the thickness of the thread you are using, so the thread passes easily through the fabric. You may need:

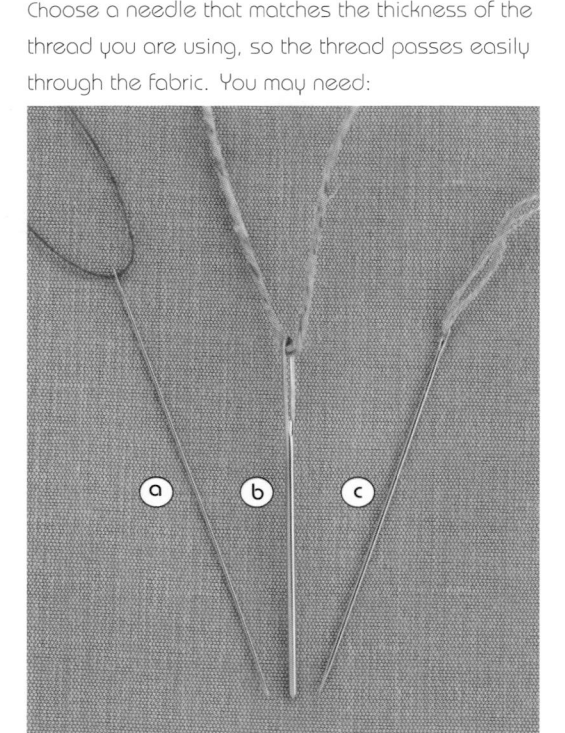

- **Beading needles** for beading **(a)**.
- **Large-eyed chenille needles** to thread twine for beaded decorations **(b)**.
- **Straw needles** – they are long and strong so will stitch through canvas or denim but are fine enough to bead and embroider with **(c)**.

Functional hand stitches

Take the time to get to grips with the two essential functional stitches – slipstitch and ladder stitch.

Slipstitch

Slipstitch is used to hem, close gaps in seams, attach pockets and to insert linings. When worked neatly, it is an almost invisible stitch. Work from right to left, picking up a tiny piece of the fabric from one seam edge with the needle. Insert the needle into the other seam fold and move the needle along the fold 3mm (⅛in). Push the needle out into the seam edge and repeat.

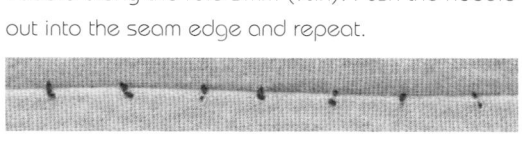

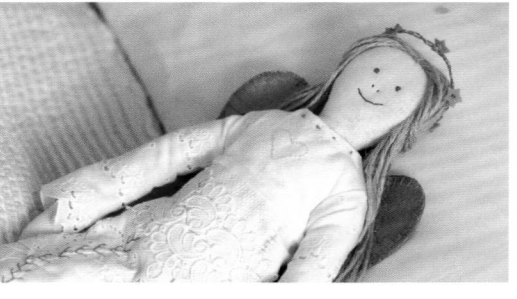

Ladder stitch

The ladder stitch is a good way to close a seam on a stuffed item. It is so called because the stitches look like a ladder until you pull the stitches tight to close the seam. Knot the end of the thread and start from inside the opening so that the knot will be hidden. The stitch is generally worked between two folded edges. Take straight edges into the folded fabric, stitching into each edge in turn. After a few stitches pull the thread taut to draw up the stitches and close the gap.

Overstitch

Overstitch is often used to sew up the gap after turning a project through but can also be used as a decorative stitch. Ensuring the two edges are level, make small even stitches over the seam at regular intervals.

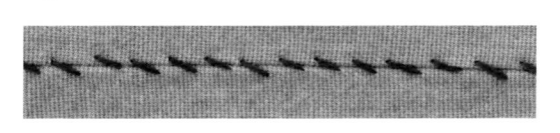

Running stitch

This simplest of stitches, commonly used to attach two pieces of fabric together, can also be used decoratively, especially for outlining a motif, sewn in a contrasting thread colour. Working from right to left, simply pass the needle in and out of the fabric, making several stitches at a time and keeping the length even.

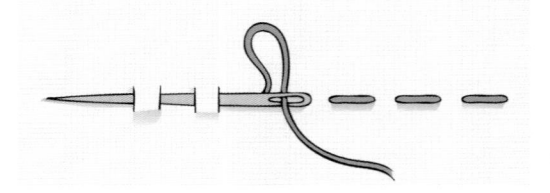

tip For an even running stitch, make the stitches on the underside equal length, but half the size or less than the upper stitches.

Decorative hand stitches

Follow the simple diagrams and instructions that follow to master these decorative stitches.

Backstitch

Backstitch is normally worked on its own for lettering or to add detail or a border. Insert the needle, take a backward stitch and bring the needle up a little way ahead of the first stitch. Insert the needle into the point where the first stitch began and repeat.

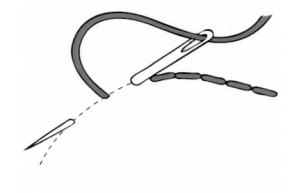

Lazy daisy

Lazy daisy is used to add decorative detail. It is very easy to work, just make a loop and anchor it with a little stitch.

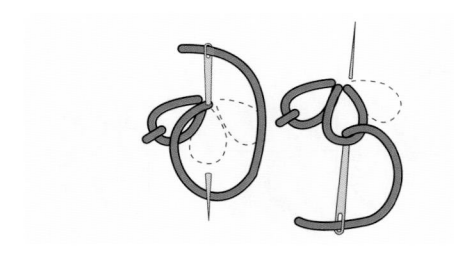

Catch stitch

This simple stitch works effectively when sewing one piece of fabric to another, to appliqué for example. It is used to attach the scalloped border and motifs to the Christmas Countdown advent calendar on pages 12–17. Tie a knot at the end of the thread and push up from the back of the fabric to the front, near the join of the two fabrics. Make a small stitch that overlaps the two fabrics in a straight line. Push the needle back through to the back of the fabric. Push the needle back to the front of the fabric a little way along from the first stitch and repeat.

Feather stitch

This is a stitch used for decorative detail. Bring the needle out at the top centre. Holding the thread down with your thumb, insert the needle to the right on the same level

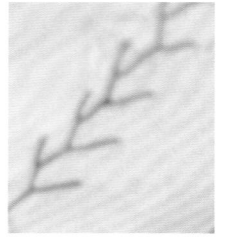

and take a small stitch to the centre, keeping the thread under the needle point. Inserting the needle a little to the left on the same level, make a small stitch to the centre. Repeat these two stitches, alternating between left and right.

Blanket stitch

Blanket stitch can be used to create a decorative edging and works best in a contrasting thread colour. Working from left to right, insert the needle into the fabric a little way in from the edge, the distance depending on the size of stitches you want, leaving the loose thread running down over the edge at right angles to it. Take the threaded end over the loose end and insert the needle a little way along

the same distance from the edge as before; pass the needle through the loop of thread and gently pull up the thread. Pull the thread taut to form the stitch over the edge.

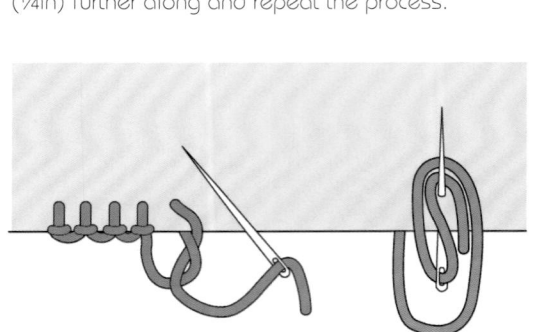

Knotted blanket stitch

This stitch is a more secure variation of blanket stitch where the thread is wound around the needle to form a knot at the fabric edge. Following the diagrams, bring the needle out of the fabric and make a 6mm (¼in) stitch through the fabric. Wrap the thread over and behind the point of the needle and pull the needle through to form a knot at the edge of the fabric. Make another stitch 6mm (¼in) further along and repeat the process.

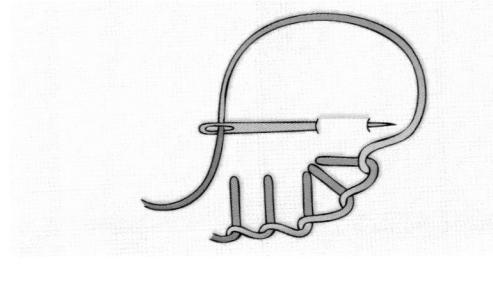

Star stitch

Push the needle up through the front of the fabric and down through it to create a stitch about 6mm (¼in) long, then bring the

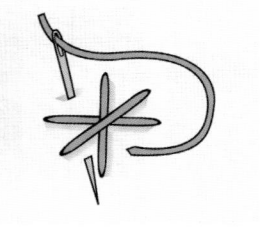

needle out to one side to make a stitch over the first one, forming a cross. Continue to work the other diagonals in this way until you have a star with eight points.

Stem stitch

As its name implies, this simple stitch is often used in embroidery to create the stems of plants. Follow the diagram, first working a 6mm (¼in) straight stitch and then bringing the needle back out 3mm (⅛in) from where the thread emerges. Holding the thread loop to one side, pull the needle through.

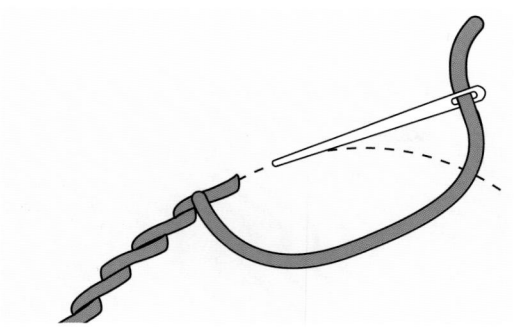

Continue making 6mm (¼in) straight stitches, bringing the needle out on the same side of the fabric each time.

French knots

These are really useful for making small raised dots, for eyes for example. The weight of the thread will determine the size of the finished stitch. Bring the needle through to the front of the fabric. With the thread held taut, twist the needle twice around the thread. Pull the thread to tighten the twists a little, then, keeping the thread taut, insert the needle back into the fabric close to the exit point. Pull the needle through the twists to the back of the fabric.

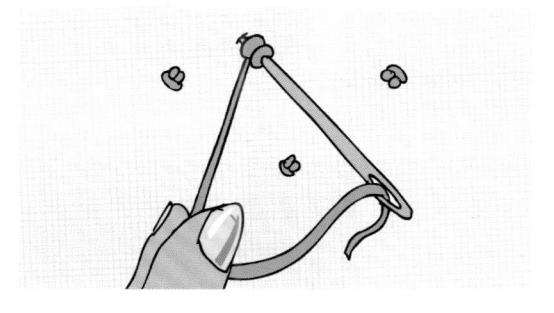

tip Don't worry too much about your stitches all being exactly the same size or too neat as a slight unevenness can add to the quirky look!

Sewing on buttons

Buttons can be used as practical fastenings or as fun embellishments. Mix different types together and stitch on in different ways for a varied look.

Two- or four-hole sew-through buttons

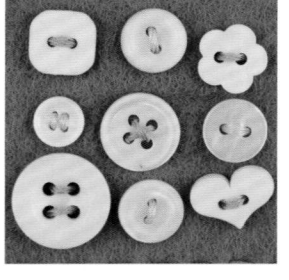

You can sew two- or four-holed buttons easily, either using two straight stitches or in a cross to apply the button to the fabric. Make a stitch where the button is to be positioned. Hold the button a little away from the fabric and sew through the holes into the fabric at least three times. Lift the button away from the fabric and wind the thread around the stitches. Finish off on the underside.

Making buttonholes

Many modern sewing machines have a foot attachment that works out the size of the buttonholes for you and sews the buttonhole in one step. Older machines operate a four-step buttonhole. Check your sewing machine manual for instructions on how to create buttonholes on your machine. When you have completed your buttonhole, take a sharp pair of embroidery scissors and cut down the centre line between the stitching, taking care not to snip through the stitches.

Sewing on sequins

Sequins are so eye catching and can add a real touch of glamour to your design. To attach a sequin secure the thread with a knot. Bring the needle and thread up through your fabric and through the centre of the sequin, concave side up, to sew in place. Thread the needle back through the centre of the sequin again. Secure the thread once the sequin has been attached.

appliqué

Applique takes its name from the French verb 'appliquer' meaning to apply. The technique involves cutting fabric to shape and applying it to a base or background fabric to create surface decoration, using either hand or machine stitching.

Using bondaweb

This double-sided fusible webbing is essential for applying appliqué motifs and joining pieces of fabric together permanently. It comes in a roll or in pre-cut pieces and looks like paper. One side can be drawn on and the other has a thin membrane of glue that melts when heated by an iron, so enabling you to attach one piece of fabric to another.

Applying bondaweb – method 1

1 Use a hot iron to press the bondaweb onto the back of the fabric you wish to appliqué. Pin the template to the front of the backed fabric and cut out the outline carefully.

2 Carefully peel the backing paper away, position the motifs in place onto the base fabric and press with the hot iron to bond the motif in position.

Applying bondaweb – method 2

1 Trace the shape you want onto the paper side of the bondaweb. Cut out roughly, and iron it onto the back of the fabric you wish to appliqué.

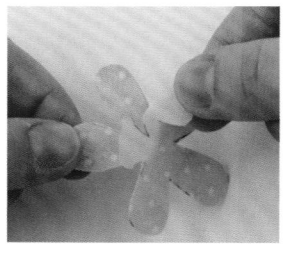

2 Carefully cut out the shape and peel the backing paper away.

3 Place the shape onto the base fabric and iron to fix in position.

tip To avoid a sticky mess on your iron, be careful to iron only the paper side of the bondaweb.

Hand appliqué

For thin fabrics using bondaweb will be sufficient to hold the stitches in place. However, when using cotton fabrics for appliqué, extra stitching will be required in addition to the bondaweb. Decorative stitches such as running stitch, catch stitch and blanket stitch (see pages 101–103) are all perfect for the job.

Machine appliqué

Using a machine straight stitch or a close-set zigzag stitch or satin stitch to apply a fabric motif is an alternative to hand stitching. This will give a secure and durable finish that is ideal for items that will be washed frequently.

The heart appliqué is held in place with machine straight stitch. The less than perfect stitching adds to the charm.

Here the fabric motif is secured by carefully stitching around its outside edge with a machine zigzag stitch set at 2mm (³⁄₃₂in) width and 0.5mm–1mm (¹⁄₆₄–¹⁄₃₂in) length.

Stitching curves

When working on curved motifs, stop on the outside edge, needle down, foot up, and then turn the fabric. To ensure a neat result, it is better to stop and start several times than try to get around the corner in one attempt.

Crazy patchwork

This is an easy way to piece together patches for a crazy patchwork look and is used for the dress of the Heavenly Angel on page 24. You will need a foundation fabric, such as calico, and assorted strips or pieces of fabric.

1 Starting with a fabric square, roughly cut off all the corners. Lay the fabric patch on the foundation fabric, then lay a strip of fabric along 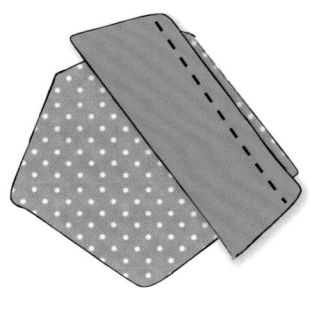 one edge of it, right sides together, raw edges matching. Sew in place, trim off the extra length of the second fabric and flip it so that it is right side up, and press.

2 Now place a different strip or chunk on an adjacent edge of the multi-sided patch. Pin and sew in place as before. Trim the excess, flip the new fabric to the right side and press.

3 Continue to sew all the way around the multi-sided patch in the same way to cover the middle section of the calico. Vary the angles at which you sew the patches to achieve a non-uniform effect.

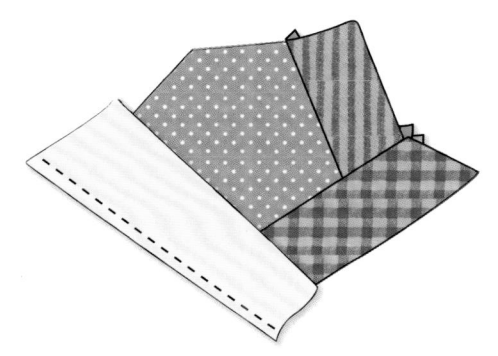

4 If there are any gaps that a strip won't cover, cut a square, turn under 6mm (¼in) on three sides (leaving the side hanging off the calico unhemmed) and pin in place. Top sew in place.

5 Once you have covered all the calico, press and then trim the edges of the patchwork even with the calico.

working with beads

The addition of a decorative beads and crystals can provide the perfect finishing touch for your projects. Don't worry if you can't find exactly the same beads that have been used in this book – a personal touch will make your project truly unique.

Sewing on beads

Beads come in a vast range of colours, textures and materials, from delicate seed beads and pearls, to large hand-painted wooden beads.

Beading needles

These are longer and thinner than sewing needles with a flat eye to pass through the small holes in seed beads. Size 10 is a good standard size, but if passing the needle through a bead several times use the finer size 13. Beading needles bend or break easily so have a good supply.

Perfect beading

When sewing beads individually secure the thread carefully on the reverse when starting and finishing. Use a strong thread (quilting thread or a doubled sewing thread). Go through each bead twice to secure it. When stitching on larger beads, space the two threads out in the hole to hold the bead firmly in position. Take a tiny backstitch on the back before sewing on the next bead.

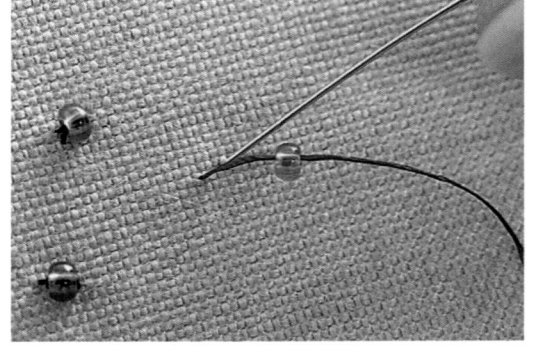

Sewing on seed beads.

Sewing on larger beads

Using a bead loom

A bead loom is used to create flat bands of beading. The width of the band is determined by the width of the loom, and the size of the beads will affect the loom size.

1 Count the beads across the design and add one to find the number of warp threads needed. Add 60cm (24in) to the finished length for attaching threads to the loom and finishing off. Tie the warp threads and split over the pin on one roller.

2 Secure the roller and arrange the threads along the spring equal to the bead size. Line the threads running parallel to one another across the other spring.

3 Tie the loose ends and loop over the pin, then turn the roller to take up the excess thread.

4 Thread a long beading needle with a 2m (2yd) length of thread and tie to the outer warp thread on one side. Pick up the required number of beads in the right order. Pull the needle through the beads and then feed back through, this time above the warp threads. Pull the thread taut and repeat for each row.

5 When about 13cm (5in) of thread is left on the weft thread, remove the needle. Thread a new length and feed through the same beads leaving a similar tail. Continue beading and sew in both ends later before trimming.

templates

holly wreath, page 6
actual size

small holly leaf cut 7

large holly leaf cut 14

Christmas countdown,
page 12 enlarge by 200%

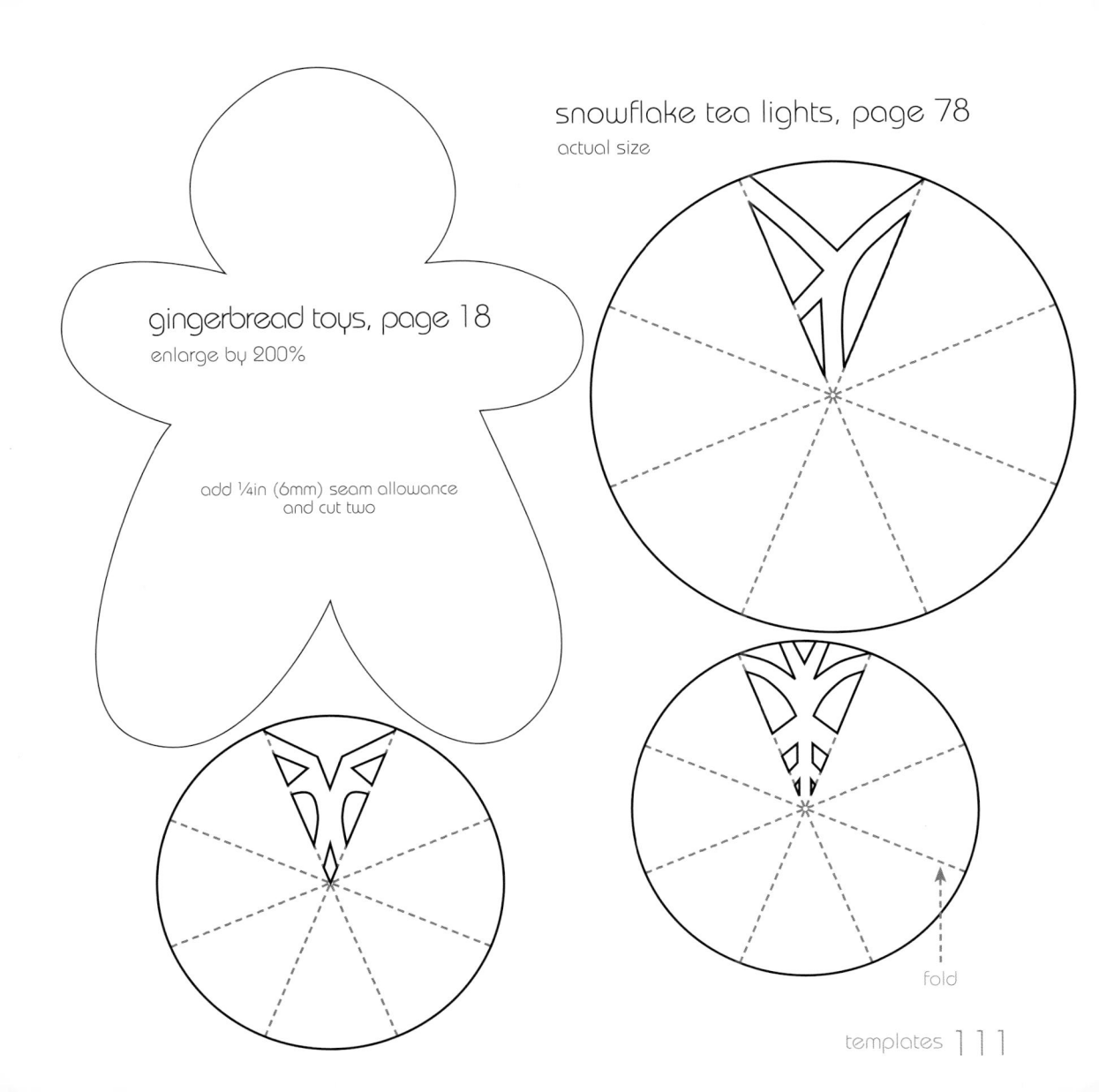

gingerbread toys, page 18

enlarge by 200%

add ¼in (6mm) seam allowance
and cut two

snowflake tea lights, page 78

actual size

fold

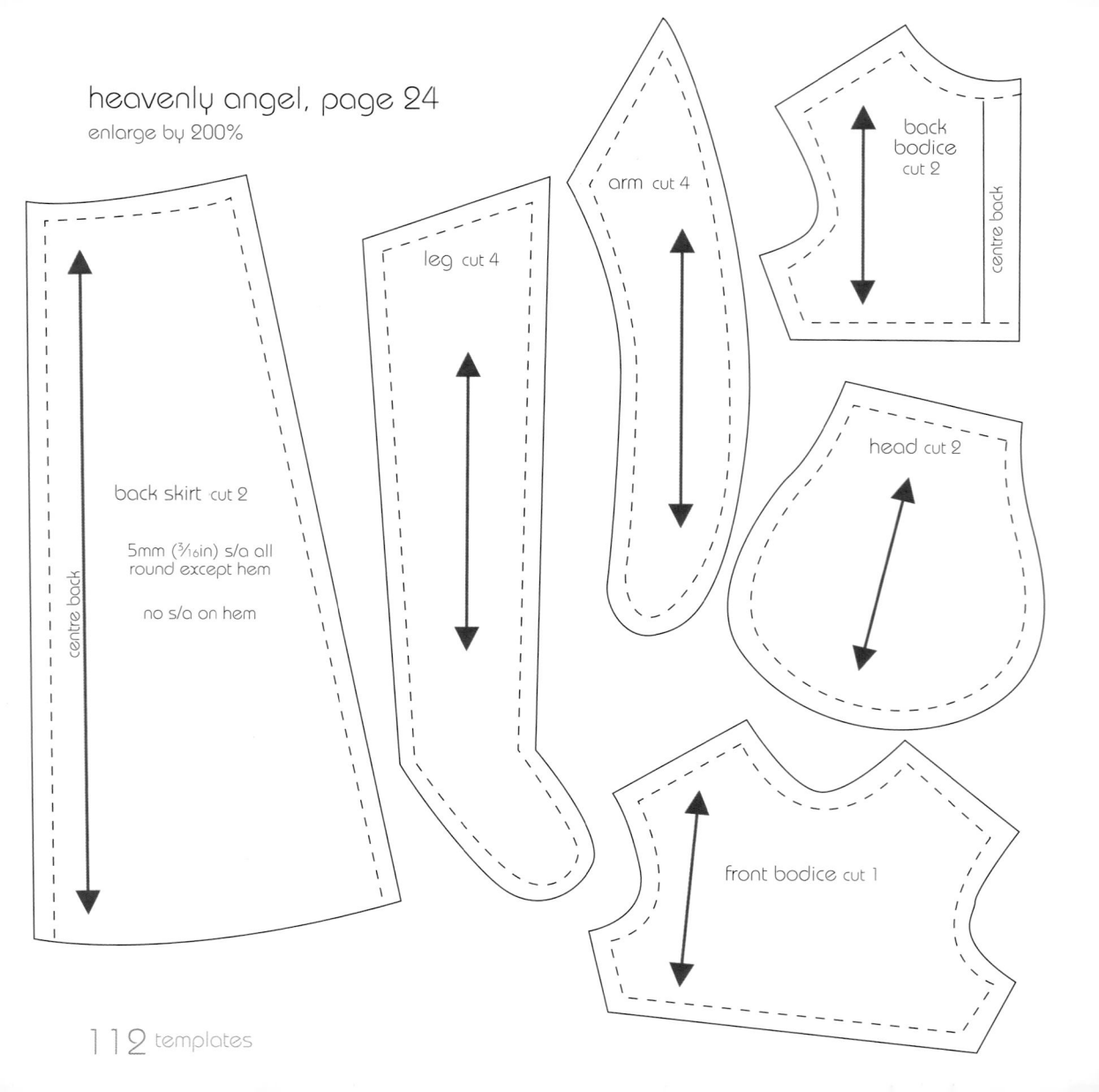

heavenly angel, page 24
enlarge by 200%

arm cut 4

back bodice cut 2

centre back

leg cut 4

head cut 2

back skirt cut 2

5mm (³⁄₁₆in) s/a all round except hem

no s/a on hem

centre back

front bodice cut 1

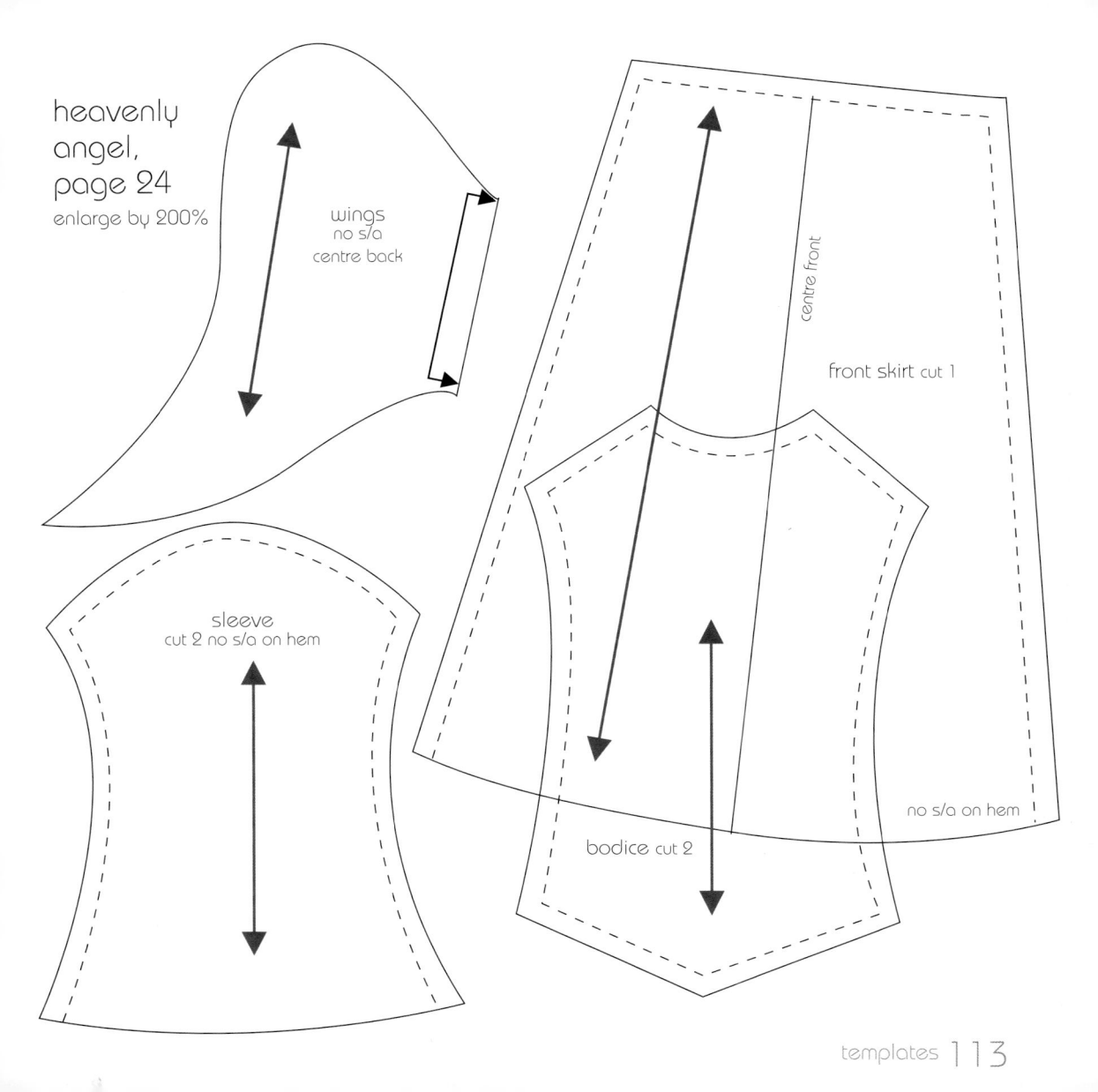

heavenly
angel,
page 24

enlarge by 200%

wings
no s/a
centre back

sleeve
cut 2 no s/a on hem

centre front

front skirt cut 1

bodice cut 2

no s/a on hem

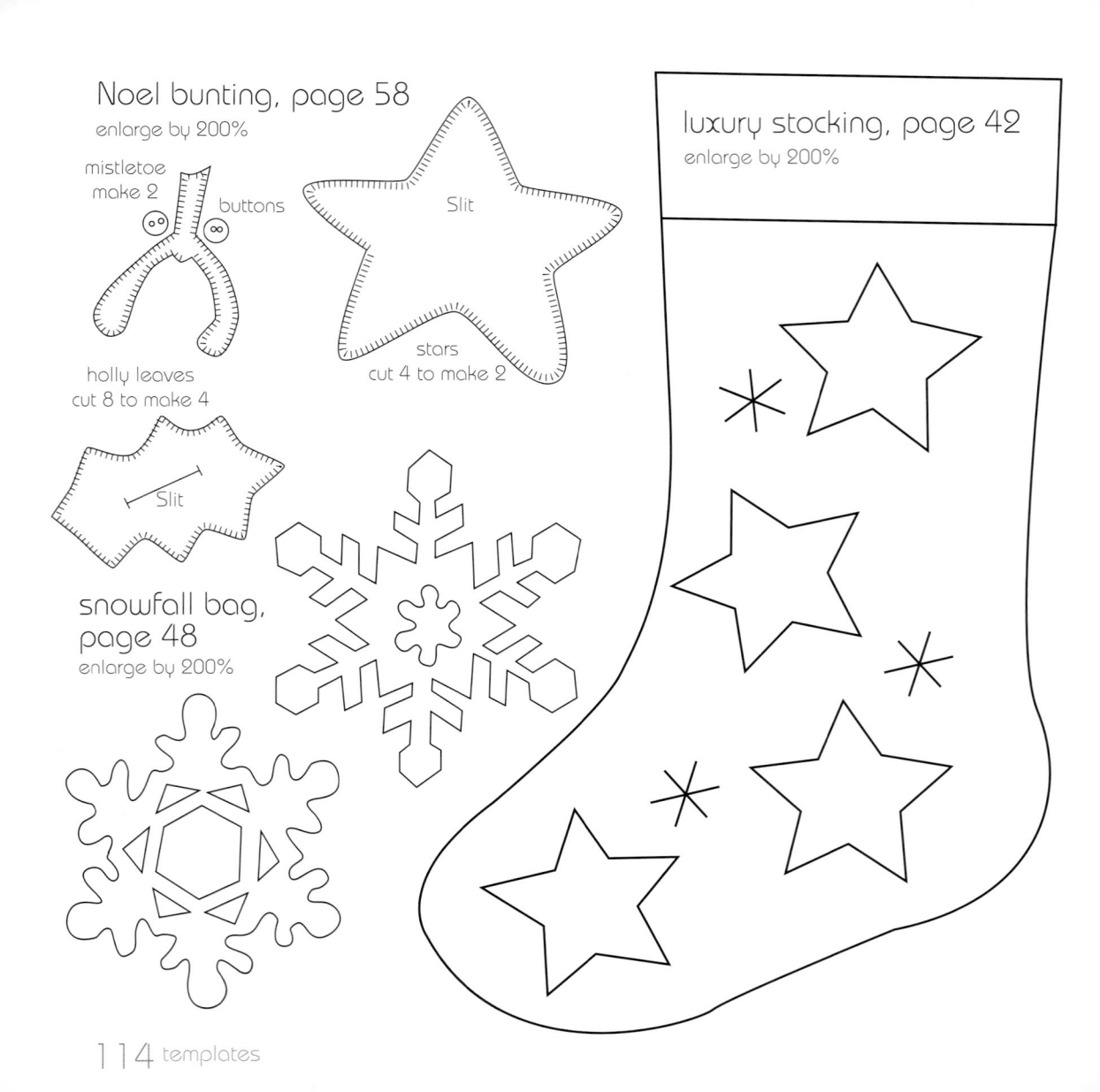

Noel bunting, page 58
enlarge by 200%

mistletoe
make 2

buttons

holly leaves
cut 8 to make 4

Slit

stars
cut 4 to make 2

snowfall bag,
page 48
enlarge by 200%

Slit

luxury stocking, page 42
enlarge by 200%

Noel bunting, page 58

enlarge by 200%

flag
cut 16 to make 8
(8 in main fabric
and 8 in lining)

Add ric-rac and sew through the middle

tree
make 2

ric-rac

snip

snip

snip

snip

leave open

snowman
cut 4 to make 2

gingerbread man
cut 4 to make 2

snip

snip

snip

snip

leave open

NOEL

Noel letters

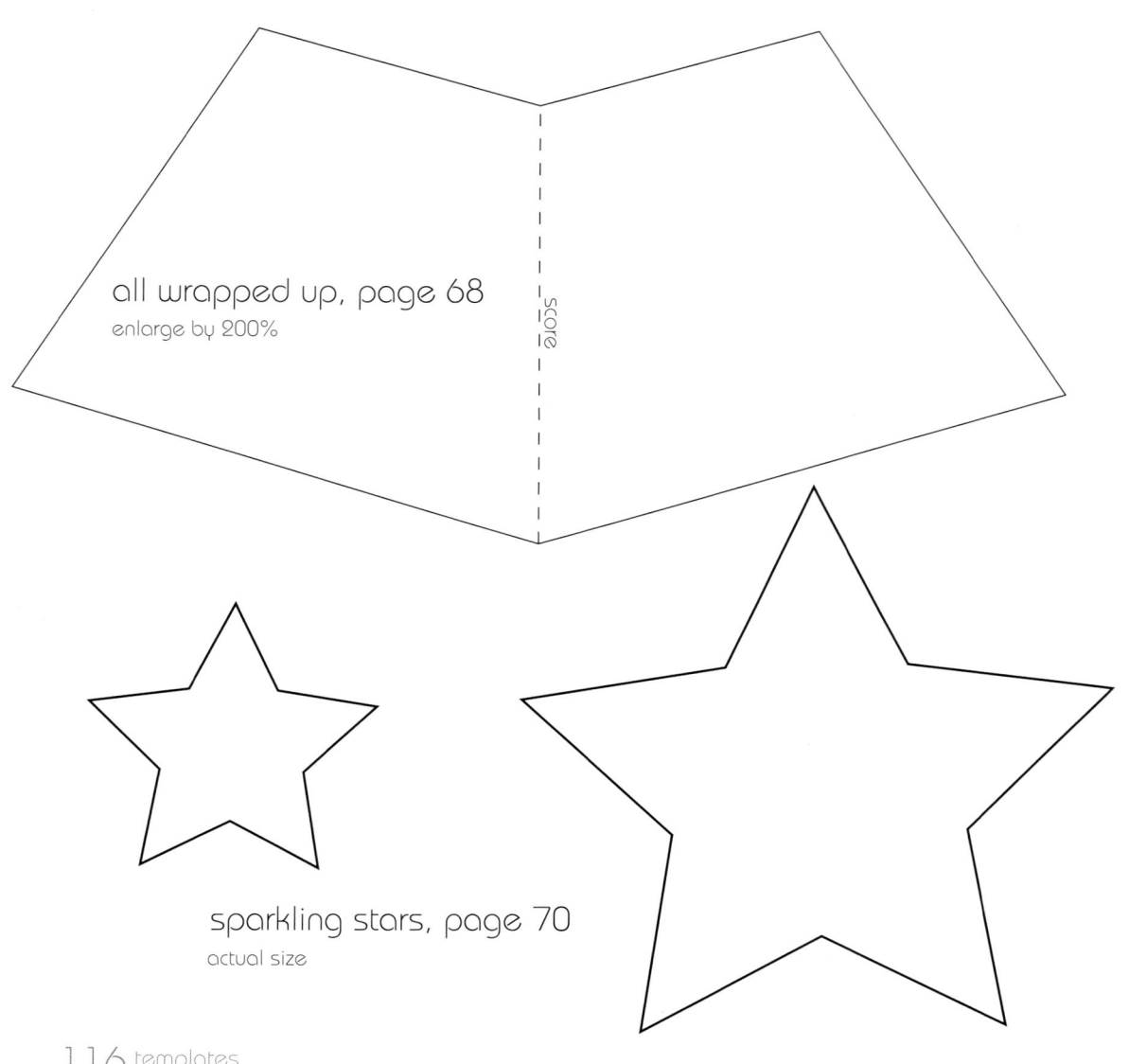

all wrapped up, page 68
enlarge by 200%

score

sparkling stars, page 70

actual size

stylish table settings,
page 72
enlarge by 200%

stylish table settings,
page 72
enlarge by 200%

designers credits

The publishers would like to thank the following designers who have allowed the reproduction of their designs in this book.

Dorothy Wood for Beaded Snowflakes, Luxury Stocking and Glittering Baubles

Alice Butcher & **Ginny Farquhar** for Holly Wreath and Heavenly Angel

Marion Elliot for Stylish Table Settings

Joan & Graham Belgrove for Cute Cupcakes

Mandy Shaw for Noel Bunting

Elizabeth Moad for Clever Cards

Helen Philipps for Gingerbread Toys

Barri Sue Gaudet for Christmas Countdown

Lindy Smith for Cookie Centrepiece

Ellen Kharade for Snowfall Bag

index